SACRED
DRUMMING

SACRED
DRUMMING

Steven Ash

edited by
Renata Ash

Sterling Publishing Co., Inc.
New York

Library of Congress Cataloging-in-Publication Data Available

10 9 8 7 6 5 4 3

Published in 2001 by Sterling Publishing Company, Inc.
387 Park Avenue South, New York, N.Y. 10016
© 2001 Godsfield Press
Text © 2001 Steven Ash
Edited by Renata Ash

Distributed in Canada by Sterling Publishing
c/o Canadian Manda Group, One Atlantic Avenue, Suite 105
Toronto, Ontario, Canada M6K 3E7
Distributed in Australia by Capricorn Link (Australia) Pty Ltd
P.O. Box 704, Windsor, NSW 2756, Australia

Printed and bound in China

Sterling ISBN 0-8069-2657-0

The publishers wish to thank the following for the use of photographs:
Jane Alexander: p. 113; **Corbis**: p. 12 Dave G. Houser; p. 15 Earl@Nazima Kowall; p. 18
Karl Wetheral; p. 52t Darrel Gulin; p. 61 Picture Press; p. 89 Roger Ressmeyer; p. 106 Joe McDonald;
p. 108 Tom Bean; **Corbis/Stockmarket**: pp. 6, 14b, 14t, 34l, 34r, 36, 37, 43, 45, 99, 115;
Getty One/Stone: pp. 32, 35; **Getty One/The Image Bank**: pp. 48, 59, 60, 75, 78, 92–3, 111.
The authors and publishers would also like to thank Nick Wood,
and Miles Halliwell for his help during the photoshoot.

CD recorded and mastered by Joe Wakeford at Halfpenny Studios, Guildford, Surrey, UK www.halfpennystudios.com

CONTENTS

INTRODUCTION

"The longest journey starts with the first step."

ANCIENT PROVERB

In this case, the journey is this book and the discovery of the sacred drum. Drumming connects you with your bones, your heartbeat, and your natural rhythms. You connect with the drum by holding it close to your heart and letting your feelings transfer into the drum. When we breathe, we all beat upon a common drum. The drum acts as a mediator between the drummer and the spirits, between space and time, power and people. The drum can change the direction of a ceremony, calling everyone's attention and eliminating distractions. When we drum, our antennae are out and our intuition is acute; and we feel for atmosphere, feel for Spirit, as we wait and call for the sacred space to be filled with *wakan* (all that is holy and sacred). The drum acts as a channel, a method of centering and projecting the attention into areas of consciousness that in normal life are unobtainable.

For me, drumming is an opportunity to serve Spirit, the very source of all of our lives and all that surrounds us on this beautiful planet. I need to feel inspiration, I need to feel as if I am coming from the real me, where love rests and there is no fear. I have been sitting here, beating my drum, waiting for guidance, actively seeking guidance through the slow, gentle connection that the drum beat gives me. It does not take long; it is the intention that counts. As I strike the skin with the stick, I move into the desire to serve clearly, and in my mind I begin to speak to Spirit. "Spirit, give me the words to write so that a clear message can be conveyed. Please let me be guided as I write, Spirit. Take me away from my ignorance and let me tell of your reality in this book. Look at the beautiful drum my beloved Renata gave me, Spirit; wood from your standing people, skin from one of your four-leggeds, and the sound so good and rich. As I close my eyes and beat, I can sense your presence, Ho, that is it Spirit—with you inside me and in every direction around me, we can write a beautiful book." *Steven Ash, spring 2001*

FOREWORD
by Grandfather Wallace Black Elk

This is the story of the drum. The drum keeper is an old woman; she lives north at a lake far away. First came the thunder and lightning; this was the first wave. The second wave came, and the second wave was a continuous noise, continuous sound.

The people who had come to seek the old woman asked each other, "Can you drum?" "No" was the answer from everyone. So there was no drummer.

They went on to meet the old lady, and when they got there at daybreak they heard the sound of the drum. It was a good sound, a sound of welcome for the Spirit-kin, for family; they could hear all their relatives in that drum sound. For four days they heard that drum beat and then found that it was a woodpecker tapping on a hollow log. So it is woodpecker who is the drum keeper.

This is a story of how the first ceremonial drum was made. They found a hollow log and they stretched an animal skin on each end, they put willow around it, and then they heard the rain, snow, wind, and all the natural elements. Then they heard thunder echo in the clouds with lightning flashing across the sky and they heard a voice yell; it was a woman's voice.

"Grandfather, it is me. There will be a time, I will come, you will hear my voice, you will live forever." They could hear voices of women and men trilling. Then came a heartbeat and all the animals came and danced, all the birds and insects and lightning came out of the earth. The stone people came out of the water and danced. Trees and plants came out and danced and they healed the people. The rhythm regulated their heartbeats and they began to shake as if they were electrified. It was the rhythm of the drum that did the healing. They kept drumming and hearing all the sounds of the earth in the drum. The drum became a sacred way and everyone gathered around the drum and began to dance. When people feel good, they dance. People who could not see were healed; those who could not walk, they got up and danced. Even those who could not taste or smell were healed with the rhythm of the drum.

We dedicate, we affirm, we hear the voice of God when the drum is beaten. In the drum are all the animals, plants, and natural things; there is lightning and thunder; everything is there in the sound of the drum. That is the way the story of the drum was told. The drum is a special gift to the people. The voice of Tunkashila, Grandfather, and all that is holy is in the drum—it is recreation for the people; when the drum sounds, the people become re-created with the heartbeat of the drum.

The world became contaminated with a smoke that came over the water; it came from the place we now call the Mediterranean Sea. The sound of the drum will clear this contamination; through the drum, a messenger can come and pray with that beating voice.

The sound of the drum is the sound of the Holy Mother. When men deny God and the Holy Mother, when they say "God who are you?"—that's when the animals pray for us. Men want to create something different to God; men create nothing. Tunkashila sparks as spirit around the world; they offer their lives and their blood becomes stone. We make our sacred pipes from this stone.

Fire was the center of grandmother and grandfather and around the fire we drum. Here we contact our ancestors: we are not separate. We can bring this back with the drum, we bring back the spirit.

All people have drums; they make drums from wood, trees, and skin. Black, yellow, red, and white—they all have drums, and we don't remember who had them first. The word drum means wooden bucket. It is also called She-he, because we all came out of the drum or womb in She, we all came out of woman.

When you were born, that is your second birthday. Before your second birthday, you were in She's womb, you were listening to the drum beat of the great mother. That is why the drum is so healing because you remember, you go back into the safety of where you came from, you get reconnected to where you came from.

Every day is sacred, not just one day of the week. When you drum, you connect with the sacred. The drum contains all the animals, plants, minerals, lightning, and thunder. All of the natural and sacred world is in the drum. The voice of God and the Holy Mother and all the two leggeds are in the drum, so when we drum we link ourselves to the tones of the rocks, water, air, wind, and rain, into She-he and He-she.

The drum represents the whole world, she knows everything, she gave birth to all that is living. When we make a drum, we make an imitation of the mother; she is wisdom. We play on her and we beat and throb with her rhythm when we dance, pray, and sing with the sacred drum.

HOW TO USE THIS BOOK

This book will give you half the picture, the part that comes from the outside to inform you. The other half will come from you, your intuition and need to learn and grow, which is stretching out from inside you. Reach into yourself as you work with the book. As you explore, you will know that you have the ability to take the journey of the sacred drum.

This book tells you about the drum, and how to buy the materials and make a drum so that it is a vehicle for your ever-growing relationship with Spirit.

We will explore painting, cleansing, blessing, and dedicating your drum so that it becomes a friend to you on this earth walk (our time between birth and death). This book will teach you about different tribal ceremonies and how the drum plays an integral part in holding the energy of ritual together by calling and following Spirit and at times leading the participants toward and into the serenity and power of Spirit. This book teaches you how to perform healing with the drum and how to celebrate the turning points of the life cycles and seasons of nature. This book contains a wealth of Native American wisdom, which you can explore and incorporate into your growing relationship with life.

It is beneficial to practice drumming regularly and develop a sense of connection that the drum can impart between the inner you, your spiritual potential, and the outer world. The drum is a doorway through which you can connect and through which you can be connected within Spirit. This is a journey that will never end and it

above **You can decorate your drum in the way that feels best to you. Think of symbols that have great, personal meaning.**

will continue to surprise you, so take time to drum. When we drum, we drum from the center of our being and so we will learn together the meanings, from the Native American perspective, of the Sacred Directions and "all our relations." Then we can learn to drum. Close your eyes and imagine that you are with us, put yourself as part of our circle, and begin to drum.

Ceremony had always been an essential part of our lives, but today it is badly missing in our hectic and busy world. Working with your sacred drum is an incredible opportunity for you to invite the power of ceremony and ritual back into your life. If you persist with your practice, the rewards will be beyond words and your life will be forever richer and more beautiful because of it.

You will also learn in this book how to use the drum for keeping your living space clear and how to create a meditative atmosphere in your home. We will then explore more fully the traditional depths and potential of sacred drumming, and how drumming can be used to shift through major issues such as fear, resentment, or anger. We will show you how using your drum can help you pass through and accept the natural biological and spiritual changes that take place in the course of our lives and which are called "rites of passage." Whether it is the joy of a new life at the birth of a baby or the gentle farewell we say to a beloved one at the end of their life, the drum will enrich and beautify every experience.

By this time, you will begin to notice what a wonderful instrument of healing your drum is and how you can use

left This spread on the Sacred
Directions introduces you to
one of the major themes in the
book, and shows you how to
use them in ceremony.

right This spread goes into
greater detail about the Sacred
Direction south, showing you
what it is connected to, and
what qualities it has.

it in a variety of earth-healing ceremonies, as well as at equinox and solstice celebrations. The drum will be your instrument of service for sacred occasions such as these.

Toward the end of the book, we encourage you to delve into your potential to create songs that come directly from Spirit. For us, this is the most rewarding and joyous part of sacred drumming, where you and your drum are one, seeking a way to express gratitude and appreciation for your life as part of the One Great Spirit.

This book is accompanied by a CD, which we would like to encourage you to listen to before you read the book so that you get a feeling for the rhythm. At intervals while reading the book, go back to the CD and draw out for yourself the reason for the type of drumming given for each different situation. The drum is your instrument for connecting you to Spirit. As such, it will help you to develop your particular personal relationship with Spirit. Drum along with the CD, close your eyes and let yourself go. Listen and play with your intention. For example, if you are drumming for cleansing, visualize yourself, your drum, and your family all being cleansed. Draw Spirit from the Sacred Directions into this cleansing ceremony. The more focused you are, the stronger the cleansing will manifest.

The more that you can vocalize while you drum, the better. In the section "The Sacred Directions," we have given you words that you might want to sing to each of the directions four times. Four is a sacred number, a circle in itself. Sing with us and feel the power and intention in the words. After you have spoken or sung the incantation for the direction, continue to drum while you say your personal prayers to the spirit of the direction you are addressing. Drum your prayers with us and you will feel for yourself the power of the drum.

CHAPTER ONE

SPIRITUALITY AND THE DRUM

"The world where there is nothing but the spirit of all things, this is the real world that is behind this one, and everything that we see here is somehow a shadow from that world."

JOHN G. NEIHARDT, *BLACK ELK SPEAKS*

Spirituality starts with a quickening, a sense of appreciation from within our consciousness. We all look out as observers from inside ourselves, filtering out—according to our past conditioning—experiences that we want to absorb. What you see is not necessarily what I see.

The beat of the drum has a quickening effect, which is so basic in its relationship to the human organism that it unifies and brings together the consciousness of all who are in hearing range to listen. No matter what you are doing or thinking, when the drum begins to pound, you and I hear the same sound and it affects us in the same way, beckoning us to listen and pay attention.

Drumming connects you with your bones, your heartbeat, and your natural rhythms. The beat brings you down-to-earth, out of your head, into your feelings and your connection to the Earth Mother. The rhythmical beat pushes through the emotions, the intellect, and into the spirit, the most etheric part of our nature. Spirit intuitively recognizes the transporting qualities of the regular beat as it draws the spiritual awareness out of the mundane into safe ceremonies and rituals that have proved protective for the soul over eons.

These ceremonies are sacred to the spirit of the people; with the drum, they draw the people together as one. Drumming can be used in the following situations:

- *The centering of the Sacred Directions ceremony that pulls in all of the spiritual qualities manifesting around and within our lives*
- *The cleansing of the aura and our home space of negative spiritual energy*
- *The projection of prayers for thanks or need with the drumbeat*
- *To focus your meditation*
- *To anchor your body through trance states*
- *To dissolve negative emotions*
- *To dislodge stuck spiritual energy in healing situations*
- *To call up the spirits of plants, of those beyond the veil where mortal consciousness cannot visit, and in the angelic realms*
- *To create a cohesive spiritual quality within a group, which draws all the participants together, in preparation for direction and spiritual ceremony*

When you feel into the spirituality of the drum, you must start by looking deep within you—it is from here that Spirit comes. It is behind your eyes, observing how you are living this life. It is listening from within your head to the sounds that enter. It is feeling through your fingers as you touch the skin of your lover. Your Spirit is the observer that is always there, always coming through—a silent voice that gently whispers your true name. Your Spirit knows your potential and seeks to be fed with light and truth. It feeds on prayer and meditation. Drumming, music, singing, and chanting are your Spirit's desserts, pure sweetness for the soul. It is your longing to gain a deeper connection that sets the intention into focus. You draw out from within yourself your "natural authentic nature," that which you really are. You beat this feeling into the drum, pulling the feeling out with your sincerity.

Where is your Spirit, which lets this manifest? You were born with it; it was there while you were in your mother's womb. Your Spirit formed at the moment of conception, and before then was in the space that we call the Mystery. It developed and grew within your form as you became an embryo. Just as the tiny, flying seed of the birch tree contains a future mature tree, so you as a child in the womb and before were filled by Spirit. You will return to the Spirit world when you "drop your robe" and let go of your physical body at death. We will all die, moving into the darkness of the west, and yet we become reborn as future generations. Therefore it is vital to respect the ancestors.

THE HISTORY AND
CROSS-CULTURE OF THE DRUM

left **Black, red, yellow, and white; all races of two-leggeds beat upon a common drum.**

From North America to Siberia, Australia to Africa, China to Britain—wherever you travel on this majestic globe, the drum is or has been used in sacred ceremony. From prehistory to the modern industrial era, time has been measured by the beat of the drum in greeting the dawn or welcoming the birth of a child, in praying for rain or celebrating at a marriage ceremony, in drumming to the setting sun or gently bidding farewell to a passing friend. The drum has measured the passage of time, holding us firmly into the now, reminding us of our heart and connection through rhythm and beat to something that we must stay connected to.

In his book *The Secret Power of Music*, David Tame describes an ancient Chinese orchestra. What mattered was to use earthly tone as an aid in reaching spiritually inward and upward to the source of all tone and of all creation. The tendency was to express single tones as clear, undifferentiated manifestations of the eminent, living cosmic tone, which pervades the entire universe. Therefore the Chinese orchestra had a large proportion of instruments that were single stones and slabs to be struck, resembling the beat of a drum.

Shamans of all cultures have used and still use the drum as their means of traveling through different layers of reality. These were the priests of ancient times, the healers, and bards. In the book *Entering the Circle* by Olga

Kharitidi, there is a part where the old shaman's drum has been broken, and the author tells us what this means for him. The other world where people go after death is a mirror reflection of our world. All things that are good for them here are bad for them there, and vice versa. So, if they had not broken Mamoush's drum when he died, he could not have used it in the other world.

THE DRUM AS STORY-TELLER

Before the complexity of modern music, wandering societies would draw together around the fire, using the drum for dance, song, and story-telling. John Fire Lame Deer, a Sioux medicine man, says that, "With us, the circle stands for togetherness of people who sit with one another around the campfire." The drum was used to help unite the people: drumming, like a heart pulse, reinforced their group identity through sound. War has sounded to the drum from the time of empire builders forcing their way toward invasion, from the troops marching to the regular rat-a-tat-tat trip of the side drum, to the fearsome boom of the Zulu warriors driving chaos and terror into their opponents. Messages from tribe to tribe were relayed, long before the advent of the telegraph, across the grasslands in Africa and through the maple woods of New England, telling of future happy gatherings or fearful circumstance, war, and disease.

Even today, the annual apprentice boy marches in Northern Ireland use the drum to convey the unity of one group of people expressing their desire to stay separate from another. The arrogance of the drum beat states, "We own the land." In the Tyrol of Austria, the regional bands come together to celebrate their culture in prayer and festivity, marching through the ancient town streets to the sound of drums and horn, lifting the population into historical and national pride. The message is as effective now as it was between the Celts and the Romans.

top and middle These symbols are powerful and they speak to your intention. When you drum, your whole being will resonate with their meaning. *bottom* Snake medicine is about transmutation, changing fear and stagnation into loving power and fertility. Snake rises out of the deep subconscious to bring healing.

THE POWER OF THE DRUM
IN MODERN SOCIETY

All of our lives are governed by the timing of cycles. You rise in the morning and go to sleep at night, consistently exploring the timing of these events. Too late or too early, what suits you and what does not suit you—this is relative to your comfort and happiness. Eating, recreation, exercise, and many other activities are based upon a regular pattern of something happening at intervals. Drumming links into this basic need for experiencing sound in regular intervals. With drumming, there is no continuous melody; it is the breaking up of silent space with sound at regular intervals. It is this regular form that comforts and soothes the modern human. The first sound that you heard was your mother's heartbeat as you floated in the amniotic sac, months before your birth. For most of us, this must have been the ultimate comfort zone and we want, deep down, to retain that level of stability.

Society is undergoing many rapid changes, so any experience that can bring the human being the feeling of "coming back home" equals security. The more that this can be experienced in the group, the more cohesive the feeling of security. Drumming brings the individual into feeling part of the group. Anyone who was part of the postwar baby boom, with The Beatles and The Rolling Stones, became part of the group. Even the word "group" became the signature for a whole social change. To the sound of the Mersey beat, the drums called a generation

right The drum connects you to your warrior nature; drumming brings you into cooperative contact with others, into a common beat.

below left We feel safe in our contact with the outer world when we are in touch with our internal rhythms. The drum connects us to our primal beat.

below right All living creatures are governed by the rhythm of the natural cycles. We watch for cyclical changes, earth's and heaven's beat.

to unite within a new and unexplored area of behavior. We began to grow our hair long and find more social freedom. These were the drums of peace; the flower children were saying, "Let's put our energy into a new beat, not into the rat-a-tat-tat of the warring drum." We went into a new and changing age with the wild drumming of Ginger Baker and Ringo Starr.

Coincidentally, or maybe it was resonance, this social change linked in with a renewal of respect for the indigenous values of the Americas and Africa. The reservation Indians began to find their dignity after nearly one hundred years of repression at the hands of the white Americans. Apartheid and white supremacy went into decline. All of this happened at the same time as the drums began to sound. These same drums are bringing us freedom as we explore their pounding in our lives.

Nowadays, we easily lose touch with our feelings and natural rhythms by being involved with mental and intellectual activity. Children spend more time in school

in front of the computer screen, or at home in front of the television, and less time feeling and aligning themselves to the natural rhythms of nature and the family. It is the purpose of each new generation to shift the boundaries and push the conditioned limitations of society.

"Your children are not your children;
They are the sons and daughters of life, longing for itself.
You may give them your love, but not your thoughts.
You may house their bodies, but not their souls.
For their souls live in the house of tomorrow.
For life goes not backward nor tarries with yesterday.
You are the bows from which your children
As living arrows are sent forth."

KAHLIL GIBRAN,
THE PROPHET

THE DRUM

The drum used for sacred drum work is, for the most part, hand-held and is made of either hollowed-out wood or steam-bent wood that is molded into a hoop. Rawhide leather is stretched over the wooden hoop and secured on the opposite side with strips of rawhide. When dry, the skin tightens. This is done by holding the drum face near to the warmth of an open fire. When dry, the drum sound is high, hollow, and hard. When the skin gets cold or damp, the skin will loosen on the frame or hoop and the sound will become low, dull, and soft. You can get many different sounds from your drum according to the environment. In a drumming group with lots of drums working together, or crossing over in sound, your drum will find a life of its own. It becomes a very versatile instrument. A group is a wonderful learning ground where you can gain confidence in your drumming. If you lose the beat, or drop your drumstick, no one cares. When we drum together, a strange uniting friendship between the drummers takes place so long as the ego stays out. This is also part of the fun, because strong drumming gives everyone the chance to learn and to excel.

Using a drum for sacred ceremony brings in a different dimension, where your level of skill as a drummer becomes directly linked with your personal growth. The more you drum, the more you will realize that the drum evolves into an extension of your self, your inner self.

left **We seek contact with Spirit through the drum; we pray and seek clarity. The beat of the drum pulls our concentration into focus.**

As you lose inhibition and loosen your mind and physical frame, your Spirit relaxes and becomes open. The drum becomes part of your journey, helping you to shift through your physical, emotional, and spiritual limitations using sound, vibration, and movement.

Hold the back of the drum with your right hand, gripping the cross made with the tightened rawhide strands. Hold the beater in the other hand. Hold the drum at chest level: the human chest could be likened to a drum and is actually shaped like an upside-down drum, with the diaphragm being the skin and the ribcage the drum hoop. Resonance travels through the flesh and the soft tissues into the bones of the human body.

Of the body tissues, the bones are physically the closest to the earth, being mineral in substance. Drumming is therefore excellent medicine for bone tissue. Drumming is also food for the nerves because it takes co-ordination and timing to get the beat right. These functions are directly linked to the central nervous system. In the schools of medicine of many indigenous cultures, the nervous system is ruled, together with the bones, by the kidneys. So drumming is also beneficial to kidney and bladder function, our ability to cleanse and let go.

The chest is hollow like a drum, and the lungs are full of air sacs that, if spread out, would cover a tennis court. In the center of the chest is the heart, which is regulating the flow of blood. Both these organs have very distinctive rhythms and beat. The regular use of drumming can help to regulate the functions of your body. The energy pathways, or meridians, of the upper limbs are carrying messages about relationships, so when you work with drumming you send solid beats and vibration through these channels, improving your response and timing.

Drumming is wonderful exercise. As you beat away on your drum, you let your body relax and become part of the movement. It is good to try and let your lower limbs

dance with the sound. The energy pathways traveling in the lower limbs carry the earth messages up and down from the inside of the body to the external environment, and they connect you to the rhythm of the earth. This is what you want when you drum: to get connected to earth, fire, air, water, and Spirit.

The power of intent transports your drumming experience out of the mundane and into a sacred experience. Intention is your consciousness directing through the beat toward a valuable outcome, like a sound arrow toward a target. The power of your intention dictates the overall quality of the experience. Be patient and strong as you drum, drawing upon the inner power to direct you.

above **The human chest is like an upside-down drum. The diaphragm is like the skin and the rib cage the hoop. Its resonance travels through the body.**

background picture **Lizard tells us about our personal visions and dreams. Do not stay asleep—awake to your dreams, make them visions of purpose.**

BUYING A DRUM

sion. The further toward the center you strike it with your beater, the deeper the sound. Here the skin is less tense and the sound is carried through the width of the skin, the whole surface resonating with the beat. The skin of the drum is thicker in some areas than others, and the sound will be warmer and more sensual; in areas where the skin is thin, the sound becomes tight. Play across the drum surface, go around the edges, explore all the nuances. You will find on certain drums—not on all and certainly not always on the most expensive ones—a very special spot that when beaten sends a very gentle resonant tremor through the whole drum body. This almost feels like a harmonic resonance. It is well worth looking out for a drum with this quality.

I t is wonderful to have your own drum, but when buying your instrument remember the saying "Haste makes waste!" It is all too easy in our culture of materialism and expectation to rush out and buy the first one that catches your eye or falls into your hands. Take your time, and wait and feel for your drum.

Your drum will be very personal to you, in size, shape, and quality. Small drums have a higher pitch and tend to behave better in damp conditions; their drawback is that they do not give as much variety in sound and color as a large drum. Large drums have more variety in sound, depending on the area of the drum beaten. The edge gives higher sounds—this is where the skin has more ten-

If you wish to have a drum that works in the damp, humid heat of the sweat lodge or that can be used outdoors in the winter, get one with a skin made of man-made fabric. These are commonly found in most alternative living and music shops, and are very durable and hard-wearing. They do tend to give a sound that has less color and variety since the skin has a uniform thickness. This type of drum is especially useful for those people who feel that they do not want to use animal parts in their medicine and music.

FINDING YOUR DRUM

Have a look in your local alternative living magazine and phone a few drum-makers—usually dedicated and sincere people on a similar path to you, who make instruments for the love of it. Ask people who drum if they know a reliable drum-maker that you can visit. Many of these people offer drum-making courses, where you can spend a weekend exploring the different skills of making and painting your own drum.

below **Drums come in many different shapes and sizes, each with its own authentic sound.**

It is the consciousness of the maker that creates a good drum. If the wood is respected as coming from Mother Earth, and comes as a gift from the earth for us to use and not abuse, the hoop becomes a good base for the drum. If the rawhide skin comes from an animal that has been killed with honor and is respected as coming from one of our relations, then we can create a beautiful drum.

If your drum is given to you by a loved one, this is often the most auspicious way of receiving from Spirit. Send a message to Spirit and let the gift come in its own time and in its own way, for you can wait for it.

If you do not want to wait, you could also visit your local alternative living shop, which will usually have excellent drums in stock for you to try. Again these people are very likely to be on the same path as you and they will have information not only on drum-makers but also drumming groups and medicine lodges where drumming is a regular event. It is well worth letting the finding of your drum be part of your journey.

far left **Drumming in a "pow-wow" ceremony connects you to your true beauty and power, dancing on the Mother Earth and singing, "We are one."**

above **The stone people lodge and sacred fire are an ancient cleansing ceremony, where the stones speak and the spirits come.**

MAKING A DRUM

Making a drum is an exciting exploration and learning experience. It is important to smudge and cleanse all the tools and materials that you use in making your drum. If you start clean and clear, then you will own an energetically clear drum at the end. The skin of the drum must be rawhide, either goat, deer, elk, or calf. Elk is the best skin to use. Do not use cured leather like that used for clothing, bags, or furniture.

When you have obtained the dry skin, let it soak in cold water, and when it is soft, stretch it over the prepared frame. The skin should be cut round and be a good bit larger than the hoop so that it goes over the sides and comes around the back with between 1–2 in (2.5–5 cm) spare. The skin will stretch when the rawhide strands are threaded around its circumference and tightened.

It is most important to sand the wooden hoop surfaces that have contact with the skin, especially the top edge. This should be rounded and sanded down with fine sandpaper and then oiled, with either beeswax or a thin coat of vegetable or wood oil. A sharp or rough edge creates resistance and can tear the wet skin as it is stretched across the wooden frame. The easier the movement between skin and wood, the tighter will be your drum skin and the better the sound.

Thread rawhide ropes (cut from the hide) through the edge of the skin as it circles the back of the drum—not too close, since it may tear—and then gently pull it tight. Ensure that where the wet drum skin meets the tightening rawhide ropes, the holes are not too near the edge of the skin. I usually thread rawhide through the prepared holes so that the pressure of the stretching is even.

above **Making a drum is a living, learning process. It brings you into contact with strength and gentleness; as you pray, your intention enters the drum.**

The best time to prepare and make the holes is when the skin has been soaked in cold water. Dry the skin with a towel and lay it on a flat surface. With a red pen, mark the positions of the first four holes in a cross signifying the Sacred Directions, ensuring a balance that is practical when it is stretched later and visually pleasing. Red is a good color because it is bright and cheerful. Then mark in each quadrant three more holes, all evenly spaced. Now you should have 16 holes marked. Do not cut the holes yet, but lay the skin over the wooden hoop and look at it for a while. Move it around and feel where the skin and wood fit and feel comfortable together. Remember or mark this position. This is a good time to make sure that the holes are not too close to the edge of the skin, since it may tear, and not too far in toward the center of the drum, since the holes will then sit like an open wound within the circle of the hoop.

Take a close look at the marked holes, checking for weak areas. When you are really satisfied that you have

MAKING A DRUM

You will need rawhide skin and a round hoop.
Do not rush at it, be patient.

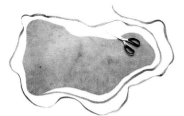

Soak the skin in water until flexible and
cut a long thong from the outside edge.

Tighten the skin over the hoop by pulling
the thong; get the tension even.

Once finished, there will be the symbol of the
Sacred Directions for you to hold.

got it right, begin cutting the holes. Work in opposite pairs, making this as perfect as you possibly can, since this is crucial to ensure even tension when it comes to stretching. Use a sharp knife to cut the holes smaller than you think you need them. Remember, you can always make a hole bigger, but you cannot make it smaller!

Place the skin in position on the hoop frame, then thread through the supporting rawhide and start cross-threading the rawhide ropes across the underside of the drum (see illustration). Work opposite hole to opposite hole, slowly increasing the pressure as you go. Sing a song to the drum. This is a powerful time in the drum-making process, because this is where the drum begins to create itself, using this criss-cross threading with the eight rawhide ropes. Make sure you lever the tension on the thread so that the skin is evenly tight.

The last job is to tie and bind these waxed threads together in fours with thread or rawhide to collect any excess slack in the still-damp skin. Then leave your drum in a warm place to dry but not by direct heat. As the drum dries, the skin will tighten on the frame: if the heat is too much, this will happen too quickly, causing cracks in the leather and a warped frame. After this stage, your drum is ready for painting. This is a learning game—if it does not work first time, start again!

MAKING A DRUMSTICK

You can very easily make your own drumstick with which to beat your drum. Take a piece of wood about as thick as your ring finger and about 14 in (35 cm) in length. Wrap about six to seven layers of material around the end of the stick and secure these to the wood with twine. When you have done this, cover the end of the stick with a layer of soft leather, and secure that with twine. Wrap strips of soft leather around the twine, to ensure that the drumstick head is secure.

PAINTING YOUR DRUM

When you make or buy a drum, you do it with the intention of having something sacred for your use in healing and ceremony. We have talked about intention as the foundation of all healing. It may take you quite some time to really get to know your intention. Think of it as your mission statement. What is your unique purpose for being here on this planet at this time? In this quest for your true purpose, you will find that a lot of answers come from your head, with your intellect telling you what to do. But you have to wait for the true answer to come from your heart. So be patient and listen. In painting your drum, you are putting you and your values, your creative power, your connection to the animal and plant world, into the drum, and you are feeling for your connection to Spirit. From where do you get your strength? You will be seeking this as you prepare yourself for this personal adventure. On your drum, you will want to paint symbols that have meaning for you, so that when you sound your drum you can look at them and remember your connection. In the painting of your drum, you will imprint your Spirit based on your personal dreams and visions that are coming to you from Spirit. There is no rush—it may be years until you get around to painting your drum and that is fine. Wait until you feel totally right about doing it.

Until you paint your drum, hang some feathers or bits of wood from the straps. With these feathers, you are asking the winged ones, or birds, to guide you. Be aware of the feathers that cross your path; feathers connect you to your spirit guides and angels, who are as close to you as you want them to be. The pieces of wood connect you to the standing people, or trees; trees are excellent teachers for us fast-moving humans.

YOU WILL NEED

- Oil paints, especially black, white, red, and yellow, plus whatever else you fancy—though it is best to keep the pallet simple and keep to earth colors
- A range of oil-painting brushes, turpentine, and white spirit, plus cloths for wiping up spills and cleaning brushes, glass jars and plates for mixing the colors
- Paper, pencils, and an eraser
- Smudging herbs and materials for creating sacred space

far left Your drum now has a power that is linked to you, an instrument for prayer and medicine. Care for it, because it will become a close friend.

right When your drum has been painted, smudge it with sage smoke to cleanse it. Sage is the most valued cleansing herb, for it is pure and sweet.

When you have decided what symbols you wish to paint on your drum, get yourself prepared for the day. It is good to make this a group activity with some friends who are painting their own drums at the same time. It is a powerful experience if you can make a happy and social, yet spiritual occasion of it.

Get all of your equipment together in advance. Give the room a good clean, and cleanse with the aromatic smoke of herbs such as sage and sweetgrass, a process known as smudging. Create a sacred space. Call in all the spiritual qualities that you and your friends want to paint on your drums. Each person should say their own prayer. Give each other a good smudging and smudge all the equipment that is going to be used for the painting.

Start by drawing the shapes and symbols onto paper, discussing with each other balance, colors, and sizes, so that when it comes to painting on the drum you are less likely to make a mistake (if such a possibility exists). Some

ideas for images you could use are eagles, buffaloes, bison, whales, crows, horses, or more stylized motifs.

BEGINNING TO PAINT

Now transfer your attention to painting the drum. This bit takes courage, especially when you first start. Oil paints take up to a week to dry, but the more that they are thinned down with turpentine, the quicker the paint dries. You will get a more textured effect from thicker paint, but beware: in the future you might lose your beautiful painting as dry flakes flick around the room when you drum. So mix the paint with turpentine, which penetrates into the skin, taking the color with it. If you make a mistake, wipe off the paint with a clean cloth soaked in white spirit. Clean the brushes well between working with each color, otherwise you will get a muddy effect. Let your drum dry by hanging it in a warm place for a week or more before you attempt to use it again.

CLEANSING, BLESSING, DEDICATING, AND CARING FOR YOUR DRUM

"Every part of this country is sacred to my people.
Every hillside, every valley,
every plain and grove has been hallowed
by some fond memory or sad experience of my tribe."

CHIEF SEATTLE,
HOW CAN ONE SELL THE AIR?
CHIEF SEATTLE'S VISION

Now that you have your drum, you will need to awaken the energetic relationship between the two of you. This has already started in the process of the drum coming to you in a sacred manner. That sacredness needs to be built upon, not only through regular use but also through cleansing with aromatic smoke from herbs like sage and sweetgrass. Keep your drum in a dry place and in a sacred area, perhaps on a wall facing south for healing, or west for reaching toward the ancestors.

When you awake your drum, you give it life, connecting you and your drum in a sacred relationship. So you may want to choose a special time alone or with a friend. Prepare yourself beforehand through prayer and meditation, remembering why you wanted a drum and what you

desire to do with it. Do you want to use it for healing or is it going to be used primarily for celebration? Decide what you and your drum are going to do together; let this purpose come to you over a few days prior to your opening-up ceremony. On the day, cleanse yourself in a bath and then smudge yourself and your drum with sage smoke. Invite your spirit guides and power animals to be present. Begin drumming and sing or send your prayers to the Sacred Directions.

As you now drum, draw in your dedications and intentions, invite blessings into your drum, let yourself go into the experience and focus on calling into the drum all the goodness, holiness, and power that you are able to experience. When the ceremony is over, make a vocal prayer of gratitude to all the spirits present. Your drum is now awakened and is now ready to be used for sacred ceremony. This awakening ceremony sets the standard for the future use of your drum.

CARING FOR YOUR DRUM

Once your drum is awakened, be selective about who uses it. You may lend it to someone to use and feel very uncomfortable about it. If you feel like this, just ask for the drum back—the spirits are giving you a message. Your drum is now part of your medicine and your power; do not let it be disrespected or defiled. When you leave the house and know other people will be around, cover it up or put the drum away in a safe place.

*"Grandfathers, you where the sun goes down,
you of the sacred wind where the white giant lives,
you where the day comes forth and the morning star,
you where lives the power to grow,
you of the sky and you of the earth,
wings of the air and four-leggeds of the world,
behold!"*

**BLACK ELK,
"PRAYER OF BLACK ROAD,"
*BLACK ELK SPEAKS***

The skin and wooden frame require very little physical care. However, beware of leaving the drum in a damp place for an extended period of time, as the wood will warp and the skin will rot because it is not cured leather. Be careful too about exposing your drum to the heat of the sun, since the tension created in the rawhide may cause the shape of the hoop to change. Do not leave your drum too close to direct heat, since the skin may tear when it is tightened. Make a waterproof bag to carry your drum in to protect it from excess heat and moisture—many drums become damaged because they are left to the mercy of the elements.

right Regular smudging will keep you energetically clear. Sweet smoke cleanses the human aura and the space where you live and work.

SMUDGING HERBS

above left Rosemary; brings in positive energies.

above right Frankincense; clears away all negative, clingy, and sticky energies.

left Lavender; cleanses and clears the mind and spirit.

below right White sage; cleanses and purifies; this is the most clarifying of all the herbs.

LEARNING TO DRUM

Now you have your drum and you know how to care for it. You now have a picture in your head of where drumming comes from and where it is to be sent to. Hold your drum in the left hand, in the center of the back so that as you grip the tensioning cords you are able to slightly tighten the skin face, creating a lighter, higher sound. Hold the drum level with your chest so that the drum's resonance can reverberate into your body cavity. Relax yourself and get in touch with your breath and your prayer. It may be easier if you close your eyes. Start by beating gently on the center of the drum with your stick.

FINDING YOUR PERSONAL BEAT

Everyone has a beat or drum rhythm that they naturally fall into, and this is what you need to explore first. This will be the foundation upon which all future drumming will be based. Keep it slow, and work on strong and even timing. Let yourself look into the sound, and look for

simplicity, not complexity. Do not judge how good or how bad you sound, but stay focused on putting your consciousness into the experience. Try halving the number of beats, leaving as much space between the drum strikes, slow and yet keeping an even rhythm. Now double the number of strikes and keep the same basic rhythm. Finish by coming back to finding your personal beat.

SOUNDING YOUR DRUM

Every drum is different in sound. The smaller the skin surface, the higher the timbre; the larger the area, the lower the timbre. You will find that because the skin is uneven in thickness, different areas will give you a different sound: the center of the drum gives a deeper sound, while at the edges the sound becomes higher. Explore your personal beat and move the drumstick around over the skin, hitting it in different areas and finding for yourself where you get the best sound. Strike the rim of the drum with the wood of the drumstick and then turn the drum over and strike the tensioning cords. Put the stick down and use your hand; try with the flat of the hand and

top left The standing people are my brothers, Mother Earth feeds me, Grandfather Sky is breathing me, and my blood is made from the sea.

below left If one hand dominates your drumming, practice drumming with the other hand; this stimulates the opposite side of the brain.

right Use your Medicine Wheel with friends to drum up your good intentions.

go over all the different surfaces. Then try using your fingernails, and interchange with the flat of the hand to obtain as much variety of sound as possible.

DRUMMING IN NATURE

Go out into the woods and explore the different areas and moods available. Watch how the drum changes with different trees and rocky outcrops. Try finding your personal beat and observe how it varies with the differing circumstances. In some places nothing happens, and you may feel out of place, but if you move just a short distance you may find that you and your drum really open up. When this happens, let yourself give your drumming as a gift and let your spirit connect with the spirit of the place.

DRUMMING WITH OTHERS

Meet up with other drummers and explore each of your personal beats. Try to listen as you drum, and follow and observe how each person is able to experience and express themselves more fully through their drumming. Be willing to let your sound come through when you feel guided; this is your opportunity to find your connection to Spirit and touch your awakening power and medicine. Explore drumming and keeping beat with your less dominant side; you will be beating strength into your spirit, within the support of your group.

"One very clear guidance that has come has been for men to join together in drumming groups. The drum is a feminine form, which emulates Mother Earth and the woman's womb, yet as in marriage, it is often given into the care of men. These men's groups, then, can become metaphorical caretakers of the instrument, the womb that renews all life and is also the continuing heartbeat at the center of life."

BROOK MEDICINE EAGLE
BUFFALO WOMAN COMES SINGING

DRUMMING CLEARS THE WAY

Hanta Yo means "clear the way." Clear away all that is in the way so that Spirit, inspiration, and creativity have a clear route of expression. This is what drumming does, clearing away all the dross and conditioned responses so that something from deep inside can come out. The beat of the drum is like a sweeping broom: the vibrating sound waves not only enter the ears, clearing the thoughts and mind, they also pierce through the congestions in the aura, moving the air around the body, bringing in clarity, and dispersing confusion in the mind.

Our limitations are most commonly a result of our fear of change. For example, pain is most often labeled as negative, and when we are hurt, we put on sorrowful faces and wait for sympathy from others for comfort. But pain makes you move from your comfort zone and seek a solution, and it is your choice where you go for this remedy. You may see your pain as not being your responsibility and wish to be a patient and present your problem to the doctor, whom you have been conditioned to look upon as a superior person. Accepting others' advice and medicines that you are expected to take, you have often given away your own power and autonomy.

Let us look at it in another way. Let us not give away our power. Let us see the pain as a way in which we can move from one chapter in life into another. Pain says, "Look at me!" Eventually you will find that you cannot run away from it forever. It makes you change your posture and your habits. It makes you look at things buried down deep in your memories—emotions or beliefs that you have wanted to keep hidden. Go to your health professional with this understanding and their role will change to empathy. Remember, offering empathy means "to feel with"—there is no sympathy, no downward gradient between you and the healer. You are equal. You just want to know what this pain means, what changes it will bring, and how these changes help bring you closer to being a happier you. Then you will find that pain is not a negative presence, but a positive and necessary part of

far left Drumming the female connection is an important facet of learning to drum. This drum is a bold symbol of this.

left The horse teaches us about power and freedom. The horse teaches us how to move, share, and learn without restriction.

*"Hanta Yo, Hanta Yo
Clear the way, clear the way
On the visible breath I come walking
Hanta Yo, Hanta Yo."*

STEVEN ASH

being alive and open to change. This advice is to help you change your attitude toward dealing with pain. However, you should always consult a health professional if you have any health concerns.

The drum pushes energy waves into the body, through the skin and through the ears, bringing in balance, rhythm, and energy. This vibration cracks open the shells of limiting thoughts and commotions, establishing order and harmony. The internal organs and tissues love order and harmony, and love to be brought into synchronicity and balance. Drumming does this by clearing the way— Hanta Yo. It creates a pathway along which clear thoughts and inspirations can travel into and out of the human energy form. Can you now begin to see what an extraordinary instrument of self-empowerment you are holding in your hands? Hanta Yo.

above A sacred buffalo has provided me with his horn, in which I keep my sacred herbs: sage, frankincense, mugwort, sweetgrass, oak, and yew.

left A repetitive drum beat pulses with energy, and throbs though the whole body and mind.

CHAPTER TWO

THE SACRED DIRECTIONS

"To our way of thinking, the Indian's symbol is the circle, the hoop.
Nature wants things to be round.
The bodies of human beings and animals have no corners.
With us, the circle stands for the togetherness of the people.
Our circle is timeless, it is new life emerging from death.
Life winning out over death."

JOHN FIRE LAME DEER, *LAME DEER SIOUX MEDICINE MAN*

The four quadrants or four directions of the compass, in conjunction with the perpendicular axis, are used in many cultures to provide a means for creating a sacred space for prayer, meditation, and ceremony. These are called the Sacred Directions, and they are also known as the Medicine Circle, the Medicine Wheel, or the Sacred Hoop. Each of the directions has a realm of influence relative to colors, seasons, time of day, and time of life. Spiritual guardians, plants, and animals are all connected to a direction. Since each one of us stands in the center of our own universe with the Sacred Directions, we send intention out in all directions, saying that everything in all directions is sacred, or *wakan*. For example, there are no hard and fast rules

above **The Medicine Wheel follows the Native American equivalent of our compass directions, but they are imbued with special power.**

about which color goes with which direction. It is all to do with what makes sense and feels comfortable to you. The Sacred Directions are the foundation and blueprint for the evolution of humans relative to all other life forms; we are part of everything and everything is part of us. Making the Medicine Wheel teachings part of our lives lets us gain a wide and all-encompassing respect for life that is all around us.

The magic and the power of healing, drumming, and ceremony is held within the Sacred Directions of the Medicine Wheel. This power stays hidden until you call it up with vocal and true intention. As you begin to invoke and call your prayers, you let your inhibitions disperse and fade away. Focusing on the symbols and arche-

left Beautiful crystals can make a stunning Medicine Wheel, which has an extraordinary and luminous quality. You can use anything for your own personal wheel.

types held within each quadrant, you draw their presence into your life, reminding yourself of who and where you are in the universe.

This is a living experience, where all aspects of your life have a place within the whole. The Spirit and the Mystery will give us guidance if we ask them honestly and clearly and have truth within our hearts.

As you move sunwise, or clockwise, around the Sacred Directions, facing each quadrant in turn, you call and pray, visualizing the colors, representative animals and plants, minerals, seasons, and times of day. If by chance you miss something, do not go back, continue forward, because you can always put it in next time round. Go round and round, stirring the vortex that you are creating with your love and intention. This vortex is a spiral of light that adds to the health and healing of the planet. This is the greatest contribution that you and I can make: to bring all the power around and within us into focus daily and to let this be the place from which we reach out toward others and the world about us.

By staying within the center of the Sacred Directions, we cannot lose. We gain more because we are open to receiving, and we give more because we are in tune with what is going on around us. The Spirits of the Sacred Directions have a power and a response that is waiting for your invitation. They love voice, song, drum, and rattle, so practice your drumming and singing with the Medicine Wheel—it does not need to be perfect. Find a rhythm that suits you, and let your voice express itself. It may croak and falter like any instrument that is out of practice. I guarantee that it will become stronger, and so will your drumming. As your skills improve, you will learn the characteristics of the directions. Before you know it, you will flow with drum and voice into the most beautiful magic. The Sacred Directions are creative and they will link you to the Great Spirit.

THE SACRED DIRECTIONS

This is a path of self-discovery and investigation that is based on your visionary view of your world and your beliefs, which make up your reality. If there is something that does not fit your view, then change it. The Medicine Wheel is a circular spiral of learning, which you incorporate into your life from your reality. It is the changing and exploration that makes it so much more real for you. You will begin to question the viability of each characteristic color, animal, tree, time of life, season, and day. This is where you will learn, bringing stability and pattern into your everyday life. You will see each breath in your morning meditation from the Medicine Wheel. You will watch your children growing up and yourself aging within a movement that has been happening since the dawn of time. You will find yourself tuning

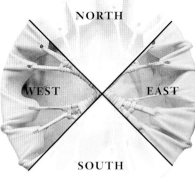

into the seasons, equinoxes, and solstices, in a way that you would not have thought possible. This is because you will be getting in tune with reality, rather than simply thinking that nature, time, and space are just incidental and separate to your reality. So begin your drumming, study this wonderful information, find how you can fit it into your life, and become a child that makes your mother, the earth, proud.

Use your drum to feel your way into the meaning of the Sacred Directions. First believe and then come to know that you are a member of the Rainbow Tribe—which is composed of people of all colors, creeds, and nations—and that you are making an invaluable contribution to the sea of human consciousness when you let go, drum, and chant your way through this reality.

left **The buffalo herd move as a family, teaching us how to be peacemakers and how to welcome others into the tribe.**

right **In the mountains you will see the faces of your ancestors. In the wind you will hear their voices as they call to Great Spirit with you.**

SOUTH

"Spirit of the South,
Spirit of the South,
Bring me healing and laughter."

RENATA ASH,
SONG OF THE SACRED DIRECTIONS

Color is yellow

Time of day is noon

Teaching comes from the plant, animal, and mineral spirits

Sense is feeling

Season is summer; time of childhood and youth

Awakens laughter, creativity, growth, expansion, healing,
and release of pain

Animal guardians are the dog and deer

Stones are topaz, yellow calcite, limonite, and honey quartz

above right We have a symbiotic relationship with the trees: when we breathe in, they breathe out, when we breathe out, they breathe in; we are relatives.

right Fire reminds us of Grandfather Sun. Fire burns away all the dross and complexities, and reduces them back to the earth.

According to Black Elk, South is the direction of the flowering tree, and represents the power of growing and the Elk nation. (Black Elk was a Sioux holy man who had a vision that started a renaissance in Mother Earth spirituality.) South is the quadrant of abundance, where summertime is at its fullest: the time of life when there is no fear, just adventure, and the whole world is at your feet. This is the fullest of times, when the midday sun lets all be filled with warmth. This is the abundance of the four-leggeds, who give so generously of their bodies that we may live. This is the direction of healing, the direction that you are always facing, because healing is always happening on one level or another.

The South teaches us to not take ourselves too seriously, but open ourselves to spontaneity and our place as co-creators. The cycles of life move on, but the ego

would like us to stay in this energetic summer and abundant heaven. The ego cannot see the beauty of things changing and moving on, so it trips us up and stops our creativity. We then need the inner child of the South to release us into our creative and giving self with humor and abandonment. In this arena, we learn to trust that everything that is given to us is for our learning; even pain and suffering has to be released in a generous and giving way. Letting the fear go, and making space for courage in the space that fear has left, takes humility and an openness of spirit. This takes being like a child, playful and not too serious. *"Remember, playfulness heals a world of woes. The more seriously you take the game, the less chance you have of winning"*—Jamie Sams, *Sacred Path Cards*.

SOUTH SUMMARY CHART

- Youth and fullness
- The element of earth
- Summer and abundance
- Midday, warmth, and activity
- The heart and emotions
- Summer solstice
- Giveaway and generosity
- Sensitivity to the feelings of others
- Loyalty and noble passions
- Love and healing (of one person for another)
- Physical discipline
- Balanced development of the physical body
- Control of appetites and appreciation
- Determination and goal-setting
- Training the senses, such as sight, hearing, taste, and feelings
- Music, singing, and voice development
- Gracefulness
- Passionate involvement in the world and idealism
- Emotional attraction to good, and repulsion to bad
- Compassion and kindness
- Anger at injustice
- Repulsion by senseless violence
- Feelings refined, developed, and controlled
- Ability to express hurt and other incongruous feelings
- Ability to express joy and other good feelings
- Ability to set aside strong feelings in order to serve others
- Giveaway ceremony and sundance ceremony
- Archangel Raphael, protector of healing and children

WEST

"Spirit of the West,
Spirit of the West,
Bring me cleansing and insight."

RENATA ASH,
SONG OF THE SACRED DIRECTIONS

Color is black

Time of day is sunset and evening

Teaching comes from those who have gone before us,
*   our ancestors*

Sense is hearing

Season of fall; adult

Awakens cleansing, insight, and prayer

Animal guardians are the bear and the badger

Stones are black tourmaline, ironstone, and jet

below When the sun goes down,
it is time to pray, to make contact
with gratitude, and go toward rest
and meditation.

West relates to your ability to go inside and pray. As nighttime comes, we are called away from our work and we begin to settle. There is now time to contemplate, be quiet, and find the source within yourself. You can feel and focus into the coming night, knowing that it will absorb all of your difficulties and prayers within its darkness. The West holds the energy of the ancestors, those that have moved beyond the veil to the place where we are all the same and where color, creed, and wealth have no importance. We can call upon the presence of the ancestors to keep our egos in perspective, making sure that we are humble, compassionate, and real, as well as courageous and fearless.

The West is also the home of the cleansing rains, crashing ocean waves, and roaring warm and wet winds. All of the western seaboards have this characteristic quality. The West corresponds to the time in life where youth matures into adulthood and the reality of your own children's dreams can almost replace your own. We are encouraged to go deeper and plumb those unseen depths of human nature. The guardians are the spirit helpers, who have walked in truth and are now in Spirit, free of their earthly flesh, and are available to be called upon by you in prayer. They speak to us through the power of the thunder beings, the sacred gods of protection, prophecy, and power, as they roll in the cloud-filled sky. Death is only changing form, like fall, night, and growing old. All life is renewed, falls away, and is regenerated in the spring.

The bear and the badger live in dark caves cut into the earth. They tell us to go inside, into our feminine nature, where we can receive the strength that rest and sleep give us. As the sun sinks over the western horizon, we can either say that it has disappeared never to return, or we can relax and watch the end of yet another cycle within a cycle and know that the circle of life never ends.

WEST SUMMARY CHART

- Middle life and maturity
- Darkness, hibernation, sleep, and rest
- Autumn equinox
- The element of water
- Ancestors and those who have gone before us
- The unknown and beyond
- Going within, meditation, and sleep
- Water and cleansing
- Dreams and visions
- Deep inner thoughts
- Testing of the will
- Perseverance
- Consolidation of personal power
- Management of power
- Spiritual insight
- Daily prayer and regular personal time
- Fasting
- Reflection and learning from the past
- Contemplation
- Silence and being alone with yourself
- Respect for elders
- Respect for the spiritual struggles of others
- Respect for others' beliefs
- Awareness of our spiritual nature
- Sacrifice and humility
- Cleansing and purification
- Love for the Creator
- Commitment to the path of personal development
- Commitment to universal life values
  and a high moral code
- Ceremony toward clear self-knowledge
- Vision, a sense of possibilities and potentialities
- The sacred stone lodge ceremony
- Vision questing
- Archangel Michael, who guides
  and protects us through our illusions

NORTH

"Spirit of the North,
Spirit of the North,
Bring me wisdom and purity."

RENATA ASH,
SONG OF THE SACRED DIRECTIONS

Color is white

Time of day is night

Teaching comes from angels, spirit guides,
*   and White Buffalo Calf Woman*

Sense is taste and smell

Season of winter; time of old age and death

Awakens wisdom, stillness, and purity

Animal guardian is the buffalo

Stones are white quartz, chalk, and flint

The Spirit of the North is the circle coming to completion. We may experience fear here as we enter into Great Mystery and may have to face the consequences of our past actions. For all of us, it is a mystery. We can go around in this perplexity and we will always come back to the beginning, back to the North. Here we learn about gratitude. The spiritual path of the new millennium will be gratitude for all that we are leaving behind, such as the patriarchal religions of the Piscean age.

From the North comes the protection of the angels and spirit guides, who are as close to us as we choose them to be: White Buffalo Calf Woman, Mother Mary, Isis, and the great woman of mythology and reality, who guides the children of earth from the Spirit world.

Endurance in the depth of winter and in the coldest hours before dawn teaches us to get close to our reality. When life is really tough and we feel at the very bottom

right Owl clears deception and brings in wisdom and magic. Owl glides over winter landscapes and comes to rest in the silence of the north.

far left When winter comes, we are drawn into the stillness, we reflect upon our past year's activity and our future dreams, and we can find peace.

of our existence, that is when we are in the North. Here we listen attentively for guidance and we speak or cry our prayer because all we can do is to acknowledge our frailty. The North is the direction of humility, but in this humility lies the wisdom of understanding. The North, perhaps more than any other direction, teaches us about the certainty of change. Even in the darkest, coldest night, we can hold onto the fact that at some point the sun will rise again. And with that sunrise will come warmth and light. However painful our experience, we know that it, too, will have to pass and make way for the new.

Buried under the snow, the seeds have already started to burst into new growth. Under the mantle of silence and death, the new life is forming. This has to be our consolation and our reason for carrying on in the depth of pain, despair, and isolation. The buffalo and the white goose are both animal guardians connecting us to the strength of the family. We are all the same family of living things and the lessons are the same for all of us. *Ho mitakuye oyasin*—to all my relations.

NORTH SUMMARY CHART

- Elders
- Wisdom
- The element of air
- Winter solstice
- Thinking
- Analyzing
- Understanding
- Speculating and calculation
- Prediction
- Organizing
- Categorizing
- Discriminating
- Criticizing
- Problem-solving
- Imagining and interpreting
- Integrating all intellectual capacities
- Completion and fulfillment
- Lessons of things that end
- Capacity to finish what we begin
- Detachment
- Freedom from fear and hate
- Freedom to experience love and knowledge
- Seeing how all things fit together
- Insight and moderation
- Listening and balancing insights
- Listening for the messages from the other side of the veil
- Intuition made conscious
- Sensing toward a balanced life
- Capacity to dwell in the center of things, taking the middle path
- Solitude, walking, and time in nature's stillness
- Justice and purity
- White Buffalo Calf Woman, Archangel Gabriel, Mother Mary
- Spirit guides, spirit helpers, and angels
- The sacred pipe ceremony

EAST

Color is red

Time of day is the sunrise

Teaching comes from the living teachers

Sense is sight

Season of spring, conception, gestation, and birth

Awakens new beginnings and conception of life and ideas

Animal guardians are the eagle and the hawk

Stones are rose quartz, jasper, carnelian, and ruby

During sleep, our Spirit travels through dreams and into other spaces and times, and as we wake each morning from our sleep, we return to be anchored in our physical temple. The rising of the red sun in the eastern sky reminds us of the new opportunities and challenges that each new day holds for us. This living moment has never been here before, and as we breathe, each breath is a new moment of challenge. The living masters (Dalai Lama, for example) all remind us of how precious each living moment is, and how each one of us

*"Spirit of the East,
Spirit of the East,
Help the new dawn in me rising."*

**RENATA ASH,
SONG OF THE SACRED DIRECTIONS**

EAST SUMMARY CHART

- Light
- New beginnings
- Renewal
- Spring equinox
- The element of fire
- Innocence
- Conception
- Guilelessness
- Spontaneity and joy
- Capacity to believe in the unseen
- Warmth of spirit
- Purity, trust, and hope
- Uncritical acceptance of others
- Love that is innocent and does not question others
- Courage and truthfulness
- Birth, childhood, and rebirth
- Illumination and optimism
- Guidance and leadership
- Beautiful speech
- The gift of sight
- Vulnerability and receptivity
- Ability to see through complex situations
- Watching over and guiding others
- Seeing situations in perspective
- Seeing hope for the people
- Seeing trust in your own vision
- Looking for the new in all situations
- Ability to focus on the present tasks
- Focus and concentration
- Devotion to the service of others
- Calling on and learning from the living teachers
- Fire ceremony and naming ceremony
- Archangel Uriel, who guides learning and awakening

has the potential to stand in our own power as an enlightened being. This is the realm of conception of new life, inspiration of the spirit, meditation on our inner and higher truth, and development of personal power. This is where we anchor ourselves in the truth before the craziness of our everyday lives takes us over.

As the soft warmth of spring pushes through the hardness of winter, there comes a rising response from all of nature; waves of flowers blossom and fall away for others to take their place. The sap rises from earth to heaven and the trees sway to the smile in the breeze. All the senses are filled with this beauty, but especially the eyes. Like those of the eagle and the hawk, whose vision is so acute that they can see a mouse move from above the clouds, our inner and outer eyes can see in ever-increasing depth.

For Grandfather Black Elk, the East corresponds to the daybreak star, the star of understanding. This early morning, the break of day, is the time to stand with the sacred drum and give thanks for this gift of life.

left **The darkest time is just before dawn. The sun is rising in all of our lives. As dawn breaks, we are awakening out of darkness.**

GRANDMOTHER EARTH

"Grandmother Earth,
Grandmother Earth,
You give me food and shelter."

RENATA ASH,
SONG OF THE SACRED DIRECTIONS

Direction is down
Color is green
Time of day is all the time
Teaching comes from cleanliness and respect
Awakens understanding and completeness
Guardians are the earth spirits Gaia and Pan

We stand on the earth, we stand on our true mother. It is the gift of the mother to let each one of us be born through one of her representatives, one of her female children. Each one of us is completely helpless, dependent on our pitiful cry and vulnerable nakedness to seduce our mother into feeding and nurturing us. Every cell of our body is created out of the tissue of the earth. We share this living temple with millions upon millions of other tiny microorganisms. This body is an abode for the Spirit, covered, fed, and supported by the earth. Every stitch of clothing, which we take so much for granted, is

GRANDMOTHER EARTH
SUMMARY CHART

- Physical
- Down below us
- Our true mother
- Being down-to-earth
- Depth of experience
- Depth of appreciation
- Connectedness to all things
- The green grass is her skin
- The mountains are her backbone
- I came from her and I will return to her
- My physical frame is constantly being made from her
- Connection to healing
- Connection to stones, minerals, and crystals
- Connection to trees, plants, and herbs
- Connection to animals with whom we share the earth
- Connection to the oceans and seas
- We stand upon the earth and under heaven
- Responsibility
- Parenting
- Earth ceremony at solstice and equinox, full and new moons
- Getting in tune
- Sitting and waiting
- Gratitude for our forefathers and foremothers

far left **Grandmother Earth is moving with the rivers and growing in the mountains. We are part of her, her children.**

background picture **Mountains form by being slowly squeezed upward by forces of the earth. Our lives are but a twinkle, a drop in the ocean of time.**

produced from plants and oils from the earth. We eat food as if it was our birthright, yet each meal comes as a gift from the mother. The wheat that is harvested, the cattle who give their flesh so that we can live, are all creatures of the earth. You may be the wealthiest person in America, working and playing in tall glass buildings and with fabulous riches, and yet all that you have accumulated is produced from the earth. This is the time to say thank you to the great mother for her generous abundance and to step out of our arrogant minds back into the reality of our humanity. And we should go even farther back than that, to realize and truly understand that we are no different and definitely not superior to other life forms that share this planet with us. Grandmother Earth has a long-term relationship with Grandfather Sky, which is expressed in every crack of lightning and through the physical love that living creatures experience.

"The shining water that moves in the streams and rivers is not simply water, but the blood of your grandfather's grandfather."

CHIEF SEATTLE,
*BROTHER EAGLE,
SISTER SKY*

GRANDFATHER SKY

"Grandfather Sky,
Grandfather Sky,
You breathe the breath of life into me."

RENATA ASH,
SONG OF THE SACRED DIRECTIONS

Direction is up

Color is blue

Time of day is all day, being aware of the power of the sky

Teaching comes from prayer and meditation

Awakens the greater vision and clarity

Guardians are the star and cloud nations

below The goddess moon reflects the brilliance of her lover, the sun, in the thirteen full moon cycles every year. Our fluid is pulled with the tides.

The energy of Grandfather Sky is so colossal that you have had to develop bones within your tissue to hold you up, to withstand the power of forces outside. Scientists call it gravity and define it as a force that pulls us into the earth, but perhaps it is the powers of the universe constantly pouring down on us. The most powerful of these is the sun, whose warmth and energy makes it the great giver of life. All plants reach upward, toward the light, spreading their leaves to harness energy and so create sugars as the basis of life's foodchains. All organic substance is condensed sunlight. Soil, wood, and even our bodies are nothing but condensed sunlight in a very organized form. The moon's cycle of filling and emptying also affects all of our lives. It regulates the menstrual cycle in all women that live on earth. The pull of the moon creates the ocean's tidal flows and since 70 percent of our body mass is water, our tissues are gently pulled and pushed by her gravity. The stars and the planets play their part in moving our purpose as we breathe in life.

As we breathe, we share the breath with all of life; as my father, Dr. Michael Ash, said, "We beat upon a common drum." The air is your inspiration, it is your link to life. When you were first born, that first gulp of air gave you the opportunity of becoming an independent traveler. No breath, no life. You share this in a symbiotic relationship with the plants and trees, which give us oxygen as a product of photosynthesis, while we give them carbon dioxide from our process of respiration.

background picture The sun is the eye of God in the clear blue sky; the sun is the eye of God reflecting behind my eye.

GRANDFATHER SKY SUMMARY CHART

- Etheric and coming into form
- Up above us
- Our true father
- Being uplifted
- Calling for spiritual guidance
- Seeking inspiration
- The breath of life
- Timing
- We are all given breath by life
- We all share a common breath
- The sun
- The moon
- The star nation
- The sky and air
- The winds and their gifts
- The clouds and rain
- The rainbow
- The sun within our hearts connects with the sun above
- The sun creates and sustains all life on earth
- The vastness of space
- The Great Mystery
- The universe and sound of Om
- The downward thrust of cosmic energy
- The angelic hosts
- Equinox and solstice ceremony, sacred pipe ceremony

*"The air is precious.
It shares its spirit with all the life it supports.
The wind that gave me my first breath
also received my last sigh."*

**CHIEF SEATTLE,
BROTHER EAGLE,
SISTER SKY**

SPIRIT OF WITHIN

*"Spirit of Within,
Spirit of Within,
You are my appreciation."*

RENATA ASH,
SONG OF THE SACRED DIRECTIONS

I nside you is your longing to grow and learn. Inside you is harbored your sense of appreciation for the gifts that life has to offer. From behind your eyes, the real you looks out. And from deep within, you feel your heartfelt feelings and you weigh up the values of the entire external world. The greatest gift is this consciousness that is within you, that looks out, and listens, feels, and tastes life. This seventh direction is the center of your individual humanity, which looks out with pain or joy, hate or love. It is the purpose of the six Sacred Directions to feed and inspire this inner, central you. And you, beating the drum by your choice, can open your inner gratitude, so that in all directions you can give honor. And since you are living and breathing into and from the center of your universe, looking out with love and respect, the great gifts of purpose and service can manifest, because now you have made yourself available to Spirit. Why has there been such a surge, a massive wave of human consciousness toward us humans finding our way into the "inner universe" that has lain dormant deep within our souls? Because in this inner space there is the sound of our heartbeat and the sound of our breathing, and that is the sound of our own inner drum of life beating. Behind that universal beat is the sound of silence, the holy name that permeates all life. This is why drumming is so powerful: because it leads you close—as close as you wish—to your source. In there is the truth; in truth we find happiness.

> *"Every time a teacher has come,*
> *he has always pointed back toward*
> *you and said, YOU, in you lies*
> *the treasure. Not somewhere else.*
> *In you lies that thing you have*
> *always looked for."*
>
> **MAHARAJI,** *REFLECTIONS*

> *"My watching eyes and feeling hands*
> *can sense your grace always.*
> *Listen for your whisper close,*
> *within this gift of life.*
> *Your love, your light, your beckoning to me.*
> *Keep me close within this gift of life."*
>
> **RENATA ASH,** *GIFT OF LIFE*

SPIRIT OF WITHIN SUMMARY CHART

- Within
- Appreciation
- Within, there is someone looking
- Within, there is someone feeling
- Within, there is someone listening
- Within, there is someone tasting and smelling
- Connecting to life from our inner space
- Integrity
- Love
- Peace
- Purpose
- Timing
- I know who I am
- I know where I am coming from
- I hold the key to my happiness
- I respond from my inner virtue
- Generator, organizer, and destroyer is within, looking out
- Connecting to all ceremony from truth
- Staying in Holy Name
- I am part of everything
- Everything is related to me
- I am responsible for all my responses and reactions
- Listening and watching for Spirit from within.

far left Drumming takes us into our gratitude, the appreciation we need to enjoy our lives. Coming from inner spirit, we greet the spirit in all things.

background picture Mountains help us to look up, reach up, and aspire toward our goals. We have no fear of searching the great wilderness inside our lives.

WAKAN TANKA

"Wakan Tanka, Great Spirit, O Great Mystery,
Take the veil of ignorance away from me.
Wakan Tanka, Great Spirit, O Great Mystery,
Take the veil away so I may see."

RENATA ASH,
SONG OF THE SACRED DIRECTIONS

Wakan Tanka, Manitou, Great Spirit, Creator, God, or the Holy Name—these are just different words for the one expressive power that pervades all existence. Wakan Tanka is expressed and yet stays hidden within all that exists. All the directions are a manifestation of Wakan Tanka. It is the power within everything and we open ourselves up to this through ceremony and prayer. Each life form is created to be an equal contributor to the beauty of the whole; this is a common purpose as well as a common mission for all life forms. We have this opportunity to rediscover this purpose by learning to be in harmony with all, touching the earth, knowing that our environment and we are one.

Wakan Tanka is this power and mystery that is there within all life and all that we think of as dead. Death does not exist. Wakan Tanka is the changing form of energy, of coming into physical reality and then returning to energy again. Wakan Tanka is the miracle and spark within the possibility that life exists in a coherent form, the fact that it comes together and works. From generation to generation, Wakan Tanka is hiding in all of life and we have the opportunity to become connected to the mystery of Wakan Tanka whenever we choose.

"Wakan Tanka can take everything away from me.
My home, my wife, my children, and my life.
Wakan Tanka can take everything away from me.
My sight, my hearing, my leg, or my arm.
There is only one thing that Wakan Tanka
cannot take away from me.
And that is my love for Wakan Tanka.
That is my choice to give.
And here I have Wakan Tanka by the short and curlies—
Because that is all Wakan Tanka wants:
My love for Wakan Tanka."
Michael Great Mountain Ash

When we beat the drum and ask Wakan Tanka to care for us, we put ourselves firmly into the source. We become equal to all and ready to learn from all. We are truly awake and ready for anything to happen. Your opportunity is to rest and wait in the breath, alive and not static, calling for the arrogance to depart, and focusing on your choice to be real and humble and watch for the manifestation of Spirit through observation and openness.

below left Wakan Tanka and God are one and the same. There is only one energy co-ordinating all of life and we are all part of its majesty.

below Calling to Wakan Tanka is a great gift from the "I am" inside, to the source of life. We can break away from separation and find unity.

"Why were the Indians so successful? They lived close to nature. They saw the Great Spirit in nature and believed Wakan Tanka was revealed to them through nature. This approach allowed them a very harmonic lifestyle. They had the wisdom to look for wisdom through what and how the Great Spirit created."

ED MCGAA, EAGLE MAN, *MOTHER EARTH SPIRITUALITY*

TOTEM ANIMALS
IN THE SACRED DIRECTIONS

In Native American spirituality the animals, plants, and minerals are regarded as our relatives. The animals are especially powerful totems, or teachers, and each of us can gain a closer relationship with ourselves through our connection with particular animals. The connection with our animal totems usually happens under quite magical circumstances, as in the following experience.

We had traveled all through the night, driving through England from east to west, across the Irish Sea, through southern Ireland and up to Brandon Bay on the magnificent Irish west coast. Most of the time, our children Joy and John slept in the back of the car among the luggage and .blankets. Exhausted and hungry, we arrived at our holiday cottage only to find a dirty, cold place, and its owner Martin dismantling his fishing boat engine. He was a bit surprised because his mother had not told him that we were coming over for a holiday. I could see in Renata's face that she was close to tears. Life had not been going too well for us up to this point, and this scenario just seemed to be another affirmation that the good things in life were not meant for us. In despair, Renata and I started cleaning the cottage as Martin began to tell us about the local sights. His conversation turned to the famous healing dolphin who was called Fungie, who lived just over the mountains in Dingle Bay. We felt our mood changing as we listened to him proudly telling us of this creature that liked to swim around boats and bathers, healing them of depression and other illnesses.

Suddenly our tiredness and frustration seemed to fall away and without hesitation we jumped back into the car and made our way up and over the Connor Pass into Dingle, only to find that we had missed the boat and had to wait for an hour. After a hasty supper, we stood on the quay waiting for the last boat of the day. Half an hour later, as we chugged out into the Dingle Bay, I remembered Horace Dobbs (an authority in the UK on the healing power of dolphins) telling me about the "dolphin dreamtime." The Aborigines of Australia believe the telepathic power of the dolphin to be so strong that, when you think about these beings, the dolphins are able to respond to your thoughts and dreams.

I put my hands on Renata's back and then sent my prayer of intention toward the dolphin, "Fungie we need your help! Renata has been so very ill for these past seven years and we are caught in this repetitive cycle of spiraling illness. Please help us! By some miracle we are here, please help Renata get well!"

far left Fungie the dolphin leapt into the air fourteen times. He gave all of himself, creating a cathartic healing response in Renata.

above Eagle flies close to the sun; does your spirit need to be as free as the Eagle? Eagle represents a state of grace earned through hard work.

Suddenly this beautiful, gleaming creature leapt out of the water. His powerful, sparkling body formed a perfect circle in the sky, until with a huge splash he was back under the clear water, only to come up into the air again with another huge jump, and again, and again, and again—in all, he leapt out of the sea fourteen times. I looked at Renata and saw her face lighting up with joy and emotion while tears were streaming down her cheeks.

At the end of this spectacular show, Fungie was spent, and he came up gently panting after his exertions, having given everything. We were all crying and laughing with joy. Renata never looked back and made a miraculous recovery. Her whole state of mind and body changed from that moment, and so did all of our lives.

SOUTH

Each of the quadrants have animal guardians and the qualities of each animal's teaching correspond to each quadrant.

HORSE—POWER

To understand the power of Horse, you will need to strive toward balance within your vision of where you are on the Medicine Wheel. True power is linked with true wisdom, remembering where you have been in relation to where you are going, using compassion, care, love, and clear teaching. You share your gifts and talents as gifts from Spirit to impart through gateways of opportunity. This is the power of Horse. Before Horse was linked to man, man was earthbound, restricted, and slow. With Horse, his horizons became unlimited, and he could fly with the wind and easily move with change and make change happen. "Stealing horses is stealing power" was a statement made by native Plains tribes.

PORCUPINE—INNOCENCE

Porcupine and Mouse have much in common; they both show us how not to take our grown-up advantage too

seriously. The child inside is always looking out from behind our eyes, even when we have grown into an adult. Porcupine is soft and gentle, adventurous enough to be out and about because of her superb coat of quills, which are used in defense. For Porcupine, there is no need to be aggressive. The medicine to learn is faith and trust: faith that we are all part of a great universal plan, and trust that we have the tools, skills, and potential to achieve our chosen destiny. We are all born with a purpose. Porcupine connects us to our inner child so that it can be fully realized on this earth walk.

above Coyote shows us that medicine is coming; it may be difficult to swallow, but it is on its way.

left "Stealing horses is stealing power" was a statement made by the native Plains tribes.

right Dog is the personification of devotion. Dog teaches us to keep our priorities right; he is the guardian of the home, ancient secrets, and babies.

COYOTE—TRICKSTER

This is where humor and light-heartedness are found in the Medicine Wheel. Coyote teaches us the medicine of the *leela*, the cosmic joke, where we slip on the banana skin just when we want the world to take our game seriously. Spirit teaches us through both the wild and the domestic dog that sometimes the joke is on us. If we are getting arrogant, then humor, clowning, and trickery can bring us back to earth so that we learn to smile at our own egos and self-created expectations. Coyote teaches us to laugh at our folly and pick ourselves up and start again.

DOG—LOYALTY

Dog teaches us how to be loyal. We can trust that Dog will stick with us through thick and thin. Dog is always lying at our feet as an understanding companion. When we have a journey to take in life, Dog is there beside us, our companion. He defends the family and home with his own life and yet asks for so little in return, only shelter and food. It is this gift of devotion that placed Dog as the archetype for spiritual achievement in the ancient Egyptian civilization. Dog teaches us that we need to keep our priorities right as we pray in the South for abundance and healing. Does the abundance that we ask for amount to just more possessions to make us feel secure in the world, or do we seek the abundance of a quality we can take with us when we shed our body?

CAT—INDEPENDENCE

Cat is so comfortable with life. Provide food and comfort for Cat and she will stay in your home. Cat teaches us how to de-stress our lives, how to slack off, smile, and purr. We all feel so many responsibilities and "shoulds and oughts." Cat says, "You are on your own in this life. You were born alone, you live alone, and you are going to die alone." Cat teaches us that ultimately we have to look within ourselves for finding our purpose in life. If we lose our way by filling our lives with other's ideas we have no one else to blame but ourselves if we do not know ourselves. When we are lonely and alone, Cat teaches us how to enjoy our own company, meditate, and be free. No one owns us—we are independent to create our own lives.

WEST

BEAR—INTROSPECTION

As the abundance of summer diminishes, the energies accumulated are sucked into the earth with the arrival of fall. They rest through the winter and await the rebirth of spring. The fall and west represent a retreat inside to hibernate, as Bear does, resting and digesting the experiences gained from last year's activity. We invite ourselves with Bear medicine to enter the cave of our own inner world, knowing that future accomplishments will come from the clarity gained in tasting fully the honeysweet truth held deep within our consciousness. Bear is strong and shakes us loose from the false expectations that life experiences are an unchanging continuum, whereas in reality there is an ebb and flow of experience, which we label as good and bad, up and down. With this powerful medicine, we learn that meditation and inner work is the central pivot to our self-empowerment. Bear loves the solitary, the wild, and the sweetness of truth. Bear takes us inside, into where we need to be.

TURTLE—MOTHER EARTH

In Native American teachings, Turtle is the oldest symbol for Mother Earth, and America is called Turtle Island. Turtle's gentleness personifies the goddess and eternal mother. The pace of our Earth Mother is slow and consistent; we are all conceived within her womb and grow from her gifts. Turtle reminds us to be gentle and respectful to the goddess Gaia, to be willing to give to, as well as receive from her bounty. Turtle also shows us the power of the shield. When we need protection from cruel or insensitive influences, Turtle teaches and reminds us how to create the cross of light within the circle of light over our energy centers, so protecting us from harm. Turtle lives close to the earth and she teaches us about staying grounded, about getting there when the time is right, rather than racing forward. Turtle is adaptable, living on land as well as in salt and fresh water; she shows us that it is good to be in tune with the changing environment and to live accordingly to the natural pace of life.

RAVEN—MAGIC

Raven is as black as the night of new moon. In native teachings, the color black means many things, but it does not mean evil. Black means going into the void, into the Great Mystery to seek answers to questions. It takes courage to face your shadow, to walk into the void of your own emptiness. Raven shows you how to contact the magic held within Spirit, when you have the courage to face the darkness of the night within yourself. This is a journey where we need to face the self-created demons that in the past we have willingly welcomed. With Raven

we can face our shadow, dispelling our ignorance and replacing it with truth. It is sacred, in the medicine ways, to honor Raven as the bringer of magic. We need to be a student of surrender and surprise in order to learn magic properly; these childlike qualities are often suppressed by the ego and dominated by the mind. It is only with the protection of Spirit that sacred magic manifests. Inviting the power of the Medicine Wheel, drumming in the Spirit, and smudging with the smoke of sacred herbs makes space for magic. Raven is a powerful teacher, who will give you the key to magic within ceremony.

above Bear teaches us about inspecting our inner world, our dream lodge.

left Raven teaches us about the magic within Spirit. Black means going into the Great Mystery, going into the magic.

BADGER—DETERMINATION

Badger lives in the Earth and has the knowledge of root herbal medicine. Plant roots can ground negative energy by draining the negative forces out through the body tissue into the ground as neutral energy. Badger medicine is direct and very much in control. Almost with aggressiveness, Badger pushes forward with the truth. All darkness, excuses, and deceptions are pushed aside as this very earthy teacher puts things to rights. Her life, home, and pathways are well managed, living in the truth passed down through the generations. Badger shows us how to connect to our ancestors with respect. Be aware that this low-slung character is no push-over; if you think that you are strong, watch the power of Badger and learn what real strength is. Whoever invented the phrase "give up," it was surely not Badger. In the British Isles, Badger holds the remnants of Bear medicine: medicine of the earth, medicine of powerful intention, medicine of strength.

NORTH

BUFFALO—PRAYER AND ABUNDANCE

"On the visible breath I come walking, in a sacred manner I walk." These are the words of White Buffalo Calf Woman as she walked away from the people, having presented them with the sacred pipe, or *chanunpa*. She walked into the herd and was transformed into a white buffalo. To many Plains tribes, the very essence of life depended upon the *pte* or *tatanka*: meat and fat for food; skins for tipis, robes, and clothes; hooves for glue; and skulls for altar. Buffalo knows that it is prayer which holds a family, tribe, and society together.

When we pray, we affect the very fabric of the universe. Prayer is energy, and in between and within all the parts of this creation is a thinking substance that holds everything together. This thinking stuff is affected by our prayers, desires, and directed energies, so be careful about what you pray for. When we call to Spirit in faith and with gratitude, our needs will be met. Perhaps not always according to our expectations, but always according to the highest good for all concerned. The web of life is complex and we cannot even begin to understand this mystery. Therefore we pray with the trust that we are

left Buffalo medicine holds the fabric of individuals and societies firmly together.

loved and cared for beyond measure, telling Spirit our needs and dreams and letting life unfold in the best possible way. Abundance is a feeling of gratefulness. It is an open appreciation and knowledge that all we receive comes to us as a gift from Spirit. We do deserve the best, and Buffalo medicine helps us to direct our attention toward the best flowing into our lives.

WOLF—TEACHER

Wolf is a leader, running ahead of the pack, and yet he is very strongly linked with the family and society. Wolf is bringing new ideas, as well as ancient wisdom, to the people, teaching them how to interrelate and respond to the new energies flowing in. The family of Wolf is very structured, the dominant pair mating for life, with only the dominant female birthing pups, while all the other females and males supply their needs. When hunting, the pack works as a team, coordinating their movements. Wolf medicine is strongly linked to telepathy within the group, based around a sound social structure. Wolf is also a loner and is allied to the moon, which represents the wisdom and knowledge held within the unconscious and the psyche. With Wolf medicine, you channel information that is personal to those coming to you for healing. Yet this information sends ripples through the sea of consciousness, affecting all of the tribe. Wolf needs time for being alone, so that the teacher within can be connected to the true reality.

MOOSE—SELF-ESTEEM AND ENCOURAGEMENT

Moose is the largest of the deer family and is extremely strong. Moose lives and grazes near water and is a fine swimmer. The bellow of moose is like his physical frame and antlers: huge. For the native people of the north, Moose represents the wisdom and encouragement that the elders can impart to the younger generations, knowing from their own experience what it is like to be hot-blooded and enthusiastic. Moose medicine boosts the self-esteem, and helps to find the right words and actions to lift the spirits. Moose is in the North of the Medicine Wheel because of his link to the elders, and because Moose in nature is somewhere between the gentleness of Deer and the power and stampede of Buffalo. Moose communicates with softness yet power, showing through his magnificent antlers and large voice that it is good to feel confident and strong about yourself.

below Snowy Owl by silent observation lets us see the nature of endurance.

SNOWY OWL—SPIRIT SEEKER

Snowy Owl moves on silent wings, gliding effortlessly over the white snow, seeking out unwary rabbits and mice. Snowy Owl is perfectly camouflaged with her speckled white garment of feathers against the icy white terrain. White, wisdom, purity, silence, winter, cold, and air are the attributes in the Medicine Wheel for the North. Snowy Owl has all of these qualities. A silent flier across pristine cold snow, Snowy Owl lets us focus through silent observation on the spirit of endurance. We must accept that angels and spirit guides are becoming more and more a part of reality, as we become more conscious of their presence in our lives. It is the living of the Medicine Wheel that brings us into contact with these silent yet powerful qualities. Snowy Owl medicine has depth and is inward-seeking, knowing that in truth we are all alone on this journey. In the animal, plant, and mineral kingdoms, we have allies that can help us on our journey. It is in the North before the birth of spring that we plumb our spiritual depths. Let the stillness and determination of Snowy Owl lead you into the new chapter.

EAST

EAGLE—SPIRIT

This majestic bird is the sovereign of the sky. Eagle medicine is the power of the Great Spirit, the connection with the divine. Eagle represents the ability to live in the realm of spirit, yet remain balanced and connected to the earth. Eagle rises and soars, and speedily observes all movement within the overall pattern of life. Eagle signifies completion of tasks and initiations that have resulted in you recognizing and gaining your personal power. Eagle flies close to Grandfather Sun, feeling the warmth on her wings as she spirals in the rising thermals with flickering wing tips. Her eyes are penetrating and free of fear, and she teaches us how to see the details and incorporate them into the overall pattern of life around us.

The hatching of an eagle chick from an egg teaches us the most profound life lesson. The chick begins to chip away at the inside of the shell with its beak, pressing against the inside of the shell for the leverage necessary to eventually break out of its prison into the light. It takes a huge amount of stamina to achieve freedom and many young eagles do not make it because of the amount of energy required. You cannot help them to get out; they have to do it themselves. If, out of compassion, you do help them hatch by weakening the shell, the chick will later die due to peritonitis. The sheer force of levering itself against the inside of the shell sucks the remaining yolk sac into the chick's abdomen—if you help it in any way, this does not happen and the chick eventually dies. The young bird has to go through this initiation, and it can take up to 24 hours for it to recover from the exhaustion before it is ready to feed.

Many two-leggeds also experience difficulty and strain beyond measure in their lives. Yet it is precisely this kind of experience that lets us grow into the free and powerful beings that we are meant to be. As for the eagle, this freedom and power has to be earned.

Eagle feathers are treasured as healing tools, being used to cleanse the aura with the smoke of sweet-smelling herbs prior to the healing taking place. You earn the right to use Eagle medicine as you go through the ups and downs of life, learning to rely on the Great Spirit for support and connection to the whole.

HAWK—MESSENGER

Hawk medicine teaches us to stay observant to all the messages in our environment, to be watchful, and to stay alert to everything we do. Life is sending us signals that

above Watch out for Hawk—something is about to happen. Look for the messages that are coming from Spirit, make a prayer, and get ready.

right Deer stays hidden, Deer is ready for anything. Deer defeats aggression with pure gentleness. Deer knows how to watch and stay aware.

need a response from us. Hawk, like the salmon and the hazel tree in Irish myth, is linked to the planet Mercury. Quick, flowing, and flexible, the hawk snatches opportunities with lightning speed. Hawk reminds us to be aware of the magic of Spirit's messages that are all around us. Can you see your weaknesses and strengths reflected in the world around you, manifesting as your reactions and responses? Can you learn to move with lightning speed when the need arises and turn your direction with agility into the area of your life that requires a response? Listen for Hawk's shrill cry reminding you to open your senses to the message coming through.

DEER—GENTLENESS

Deer survives and flourishes in these modern times. She nestles in hidden places, sliding whisper-like along curving clear paths between her sisters, the trees. Not a sound is made in her movements and yet her presence is bewitching and magical. Deer shows us how to develop our personalities in silence and with humility. She shows us how to listen and watch and enjoy being the observer of life. Rather than pushing ahead, Deer shows us how to weave our way through the obstructions with love and sensitivity. Deer teaches us to use the power of gentleness to touch the minds and hearts of others, who carry their own wounds, and are in their limited wisdom trying to prevent us from reaching the top of the Sacred Mountain. Deer personifies unconditional love, asking you to use gentleness of Spirit to heal wounds.

"Do not try to change people. Life changes people." Deer teaches us the lesson of being a true facilitator of the Great Spirit, and of letting gentleness and understanding be the dominant features of our relationship with others. It teaches us about just being there for others, without judgment and opinion, and letting the grace flow through our spirit, thoughts, and actions. This is a very special teacher because Deer shows us action with nonaction, and how to stand apart from our egos.

TREES IN THE MEDICINE WHEEL

South

APPLE—DESTINY

Apple is truly a magical tree. I have a very special friend whom I call "Grandmother." On one occasion she would not let me leave her. I stayed for a whole afternoon being educated by this ancient friend. "Why are you in such a hurry to go? Don't stand on my babies, you are so clumsy. Can't you see where you are going?" She berated me for hours about where I was going in my life. Apple is the master of love, poetry, and inspiration; she helps us to find a foundation and individual creative purpose. Venus and the element water rule her.

OAK—STRENGTH

Oak teaches us about courage and strength. Her energy is deep and enduring with a feeling of solid quietness. It is a wonderful experience to find peace in the aura of an oak. Climb into one to rest and meditate, and there you will receive inner spiritual support; the air is almost thick with support. The oak tree holds the doorways to mysteries of

the Mother Earth and there is no better way to experience the magical quality of our earth mother than through oak. Jupiter and the element earth rule oak.

BEECH—WISDOM AND TOLERANCE

Beech is said to be the book of the past. It is linked to all written and oral wisdom, helping us find the connective wisdom of the past to place into our future. Beech has the magic of wishes, so you might want to take a piece of the wood, scratch your wish onto it, bury it in a chosen place, and then wait. Beech helps us to be more tolerant and enables us to let go of fixed ideas. Beech also teaches us how to clean up our act, by keeping a clear space. Saturn rules beech under the elements of earth and air.

West

MAPLE—GENEROSITY AND GIVING

Maple in the fall displays a beauty that shines and glows, bringing joy and laughter into the hearts of all. This elegant tree loves us humans with such intensity; in a sense, she is the tree nearest to being human. The native people call trees "standing people," and with good reason

left The roots of the trees pull minerals from those that have passed this way before you. In trees you will see the faces of your ancestors.

above Sit with a tree in silence, while you listen, watch, and wait. In the rustling and creaking are spirit voices that are singing to you.

when it comes to maple. Here you will find easy and accessible communication, since this tree has such an affinity for us "two-leggeds." In early spring, this wonderful tree once again gives us the gift of her sweet sap. What selfless generosity she displays toward us. She comes under Jupiter and the element earth. Maple teaches us about fun and generosity, of how to give without measure, and how to "give away." When we give, we empty out the past accumulations, so that the new can flow into the space provided.

WILLOW—FLEXIBILITY

Willow teaches us how to flow through life; no matter how much we are pushed down and washed away, we can still reroot ourselves into the stream of life. Willow is ruled by the moon and always grows near water. She helps us to gain the gift of night visions and is especially good at helping us to connect with our spirit guides. I met my spirit guide White Feather during an experience in a willow tree. Willow is used for making the stone people lodge or sweat lodge because she bends so willingly. Willow wands are used for divining water and she helps us to divine the psyche in others and the group. Willow will also help you to trust your intuition and inner feelings.

"Fluttering eyes slip through maples so green,
The prettiest sight that you have ever seen,
But she's gone, gone with the summer breeze
To return with new leaves."

STEVEN ASH

North

PINE—CLEANSING

This beautiful sentinel marches over the mountain ranges, bringing pure fresh air and cleansing resinous scents into the humid valleys. Because pine cones grow in a spiral pattern on the branches, they were thought to be good conductors of magical energy. Pine cones were used in fertility rites, and pine resin is burned to clear negative energies, being said to repel evil and return negative energy to its source. Pine teaches us about foresight, showing us a way into the future. She reminds us of the importance of taking an overview, encouraging objectivity, and farsightedness. She prepares us for the future, which is why her tissues are so linked with cleansing and purification. A silent and ancient teacher, who knows how to survive within the most dramatic circumstances, Pine lets us see clearly through the darkest and coldest trials. Pine loves sandy and well-drained soils; below their lofty air-filled branches, the floor is clean and clear of all but fungi and magic toadstools. They create a land of space, sweet smells, and warmth, a place of peace and safety.

YEW—REBIRTH

Yew trees are such a sacred joy to have near us. They awaken in the late fall after sleeping through the summer months. When near these huge ancient brothers and sisters, you cannot help but feel you are in sacred space. They speak slowly and gently about returning and rebirthing, about life continuing on and on. They tell us that the only way to be is in prayer and preparation for the journey to come to an end and then begin again. Their huge branches droop toward the ground, eventually breaking off from the main trunk to take root in the earth as a new tree. Thus huge ancient groves have become established and have been used by shamans for prayer and ceremony over countless eons. This ancient master of time speaks in the old language of trees (using thee and thou), connecting us to our roots, history, and ancestor medicine. Yew groves are places of healing, for releasing pain and suffering that has been long held hidden in our cellular genetic blueprints. Sing and drum to the tree guardians and they will reward you by releasing you from your bondage to family, race, and historical suffering.

"Oh great Yewen tree, we cherish thee,
We cherish thee, we cherish thee,
Oh great Yewen tree, we cherish thee."

STEVEN ASH

East

ROWAN—BIRTH AND ENLIVENING

The rowan is a tree of spring and fall, and is linked to the sun and fire. She will protect you against enchantment. Rowan is often found growing close to sacred sites and ley or energy lines. The magic of this tree is of the highest and purest; another name for it is quickbeam. She heals psychic powers where they are damaged and is a bringer of success.

ASH—REBIRTH, HEALING, AND THE SEA

The power of ash is based around linking the inner and outer worlds. She is known as the "marriage bed of opposites." I have found ash has been very supportive in my marriage, encouraging me to release my fears of being overpowered and dominated; she always has encouraged me to enjoy my freedom and yet give love freely and openly without judgment or reserve. This is a tree of the Aquarian age, of clear thinking, and water. Ash is ruled by the sun and yet is connected strongly to the flow of water. My father's native name was Great Mountain Ash.

SILVER BIRCH—THE FAMILY

The beautiful silver birch heralds new beginnings and shows us how to value new life entering the family circle. Her medicine draws family members together, letting them feel safe within the closeness and intimacy that the family offers. Her dryad, or elemental spirit, is of the young goddess. She is a powerful healer, especially for the Spirit when it is down or feeling stuck. Silver birch is ruled by the planet Venus.

background picture Pine trees bring purification. Their needles make a wonderful, warming drink, which will cleanse your blood and body fluids.

right Look closely at the bark of the birch and you will see shimmering rainbows. We are the rainbow people, the trees are our relatives.

TREE DRUMMING EXERCISES

Your drum is a wonderful tool that can help you connect to the power and wisdom of trees. Make it a priority to go out into nature as often as possible, finding yourself a quiet and undisturbed place where you can start drumming and singing without feeling self-conscious. The trees do not judge—they just listen to the words between the words, the truth that cannot be spoken but wings its way out of your heart through your drumbeat and song. Do not be impatient in demanding an answer from these ancient friends. The trees will speak to you when the time is right and when they are sure that you are open enough to hear what they have got to say.

TREE DRUMMING
Exercise 1

❖ Go to a grove of trees with which you feel a relationship.

❖ Speak to the trees with open arms and introduce your intention to the grove.

❖ Select one tree and, touching the bark with your right hand, walk clockwise around the tree three times.

❖ Stop in the North and rest your forehead against the tree, sending your respect and intention right out into the tree's body.

❖ Close your eyes and watch for the tree's life force with your third eye—slow your breathing down until you are fully alert to the tree's consciousness.

❖ Turn and rest the whole of your back against the tree as you sit down.

❖ Slowly begin to drum gently and respectfully. Remember that trees do not like loud noises. Seek the tree's song and melody. Stay with this sound and enter

left These 3,000-year-old yew trees come alive in the winter months. If I am humble, I may learn from their wisdom.

far left "Spirit of the grove, please teach me how to be. When I am gone, you will still be here. I will sing through you in whispering winds."

with your consciousness into the tree's medicine. Ask, and the tree will willingly answer—often I find they use the old English forms, replying "thee" and "thou."

❖ When you have finished, thank the tree and leave a gift for the tree, such as a stone or some herbs. You will find that you will always have a strong affinity to this tree after giving of yourself in this manner.

TREE DRUMMING
Exercise 2

❖ Walk toward the tree that you wish to talk to. As you near the tree you have chosen, feel with your hands for the tree's energy field or aura.

❖ Stand just within this energy field, then bend your knees slightly and lift your arms toward the sky.

❖ When you do this, feel your feet become the tree's roots, your legs and body become the tree's trunk, and your arms become the tree's branches.

❖ Looking at the tree, unfocus your eyes, and watch with a visioning gaze (unfocused watching) all around you.

❖ Breathe toward the tree, sending your intention and your friendship toward the tree.

❖ Lower your hands and pick up your drum.

❖ Begin drumming while gazing, seeking the rhythm and song of the tree. Look for the tree's face.

❖ You will break the spell if you focus your eyes, so keep your vision unfocused, no matter what happens.

❖ Pray and sing to the tree, moving and flowing with this quiet, strong relative.

❖ When you feel a sense of welcome, go closer to the tree and, circling clockwise, sing the tree's song or the song of the Sacred Directions.

❖ Close your eyes and wait.

❖ When you have finished, thank the tree for the experience, then leave a gift and move away.

Oh great Yewen tree, I cherish thee, I cherish thee.

TOTEM MINERALS
OF THE MEDICINE WHEEL

The stone people are the record-keepers for our Mother Earth. These wonderful, silent, and very still teachers can give us seekers knowledge about the history of our beautiful planet and her children. The stone people's mission of service is holding and directing energy. The external skin of the earth is made of rock, which has been shifted by earth movements, weathered by storms and ocean waves, rolled and ground down by glaciers, cracked by ice, and smoothed to a fine polish by streams and rivers. Rocks hold the memory of the land, and there is a saying, "If you have a question, ask a stone." Rocks carry records of earth changes and transport electromagnetic energy on the mother's surface. The stone people collect the energy and hold it for later use.

It has been found over the centuries within a variety of cultures that different minerals hold and conduit different energetic characteristics. Minerals, crystals, and stones also absorb energy impulses, which means they can be programmed with information. You can program stones to hold the sacred energy of the Medicine Wheel and place them in Mother Earth at the numerous sacred sites that have been neglected. With your drum and rattle, visit these precious places and perform your ceremony, then pray to the spirit of the land on which you live. Make gifts to the land of blessed stones that have been cleansed, resanctified, and made sacred with your intent. For too long, we have treated the earth as tourists, separating ourselves, severing our connection with our true mother, the physical and feeling world of the earth, and choosing not to recognize our connection to our true father, sourced within the energy of prayer and meditation. Now is our opportunity. From the list of stones below, choose those that will suit your vision of the Medicine Wheel.

YELLOW STONES USED IN THE SOUTH

Citrine is a yellow crystal quartz. This mineral encourages joy and happiness, and helps overcome depression. Citrine encourages the desire for variety, new experiences, and self-realization.

Orange Calcite has a strong effect on speeding up development, especially in children, but also in adults who have lost hope in good things happening in their lives.

BLACK STONES USED IN THE WEST

Black Obsidian helps us to attain integrity by enabling us to see our shadow sides in their true nature. It dissolves shocks, fears, trauma, and blocks. It is used for removing obsessions and for protection against psychic attack.

Black Tourmaline is the most protective and grounding of the minerals. It is used for relieving electromagnetic stress, and it encourages balance and a relaxed attitude. This mineral discharges tension from our bodies and protects us from negative stress and energy.

WHITE STONES USED IN THE NORTH

Clear Quartz is used for balance, focus, and clarity. This mineral clarifies our view of our own true nature and helps us to overcome our mental limitations.

Milky Quartz has the same action as Clear Quartz, but it is more gentle, less directing, and more balancing. This mineral is used for bringing balance and purity into our thoughts and personal vision.

RED STONES USED IN THE EAST

Carnelian is a beautiful orange-yellow, iron-based quartz. It encourages steadfastness and community spirit, promoting courage to stand up to everyday difficulties.

Red Jasper is a fine-grained quartz. It is used to help you become more determined in achieving your goals and transforming ideas into actions. Red Jasper is used for protection and grounding.

STONES USED FOR MOTHER EARTH

Turquoise helps us to recognize why we make choices, and to accept that we create our own destiny. It helps us to overcome exhaustion and a self-blaming attitude.

Aventurine reveals to us what makes us happy or unhappy. It stimulates dreaming and helps our self-determination and individuality. It makes us more tolerant to anger and disturbance, keeping us calm and relaxed.

STONES USED FOR GRANDFATHER SKY

Bluelace agate gives protection, security, and safety by resolving tension. It supports spiritual growth and inner retreat. It encourages a calm and contemplative attitude, helping us to digest life experiences.

Chalcedony helps us in our ability to listen and understand, as well as to communicate effectively. It encourages the pleasure of communication with humans, animals, plants, minerals, and beings from other worlds.

below Minerals all vibrate at different frequencies and so adjust the subtle energies of the human being. "If you have a question, ask a stone" is an ancient Native saying.

DRUMMING INTO OUR HOLLOWNESS

HOLLOW HARVEST.

I drum to you, I feel so hollow,
Want to cry—no tears will come.
I am the child, you are my guidance.
I stand and wait for you to come.

This humble shell can only echo
That true song your breath can give
To breathe in you and feel you calling
Me into your knowledge

I stand, my arms are stretched wide open.
Face the sea, I call to you.
I walk to you, I have no other,
Drumming, calling, serving you

Humble soul alone can cherish
Precious gift that all desire.
Beyond all form Creator is calling
All who need this knowledge

In your sky a cloud can wander,
In this life I am the same,
To breathe in you
Into your Harvest, in my life of Holy Name

Constant breath of life is brimming
In my true reality.
Can I stay within your harvest?
Stay in Spirit in me, and there be free.

STEVEN ASH

The drum beats a hollow prayer, a prayer based upon searching the void that each of us holds within our individual human frame. With the drum, we search, finding the relationship between our external experience and our inner reality. The more we can identify and resonate with the allies that Spirit has put on our path, the more we can find our power and identity as true, authentic humans.

Allies in the animal, plant, and mineral kingdoms surround us. Our relationship to these allies is often very personal, but their closeness may be elusive and inexplicable. The ancient people had a close relationship to their relations in these kingdoms, seeing them as portents and bringing with them opportunities for learning deeper wisdom. When a strong spiritual, emotional, or physical understanding occurred, this was related to the Sacred Directions of the Medicine Wheel. The understanding of the circle of life became clearer as each experience was incorporated into the life journey.

With the drum, we can now explore this ancient wisdom. Watching the world about us with our eyes wide open, we become observers to the teaching of Spirit. The drum gives us a rhythm to coordinate our senses to, taking us into the realm of magic where we can find our personal timing, listening more closely to the greater reality of Spirit. Listening is linked with the function of balance, like when a ship lists from side to side as it tries to find balance. We have this joint mechanism of balance and listening in the inner ear, as well as hearing and timing and rhythm.

As we beat the hollowness of the drum, we can attune our inner world to the animal, plant, and mineral kingdoms, finding where they fit into the pattern of life manifesting itself through us. The archetype animals, plants, and minerals described here are meant to act as reference points for you on this journey of discovery. In the same way that a ship needs an anchor so that it is not swept away by the waves, so we need signposts to orient ourselves. Work with the animals, the trees, and the minerals and find out which ones feel closest to you. These will be your allies and helpers for the journey ahead.

below **The Medicine Wheel corresponds to the circle of life. We pray with the Medicine Wheel every day. It keeps us close to Great Spirit.**

CEREMONY: CEREMONIAL DRUMMING

In Native American tradition, there are many ceremonies where the drum plays a major role. This is because the drum can be heard over great distances. It can drive the proceedings, setting and readjusting the atmosphere as required.

THE CEREMONY BEGINS

The ceremony is ready to start, people are waiting, greeting each other and talking, ready to be called together. Start the drumbeat, using your attention and your eyes to align the group energy. The drums beat, calling the people together—calling them to come, to stop what they are doing, and to follow the call of Spirit. The drums beckon, responding to the intention of the drummers, calling, calling. The beat and the intensity of the drums communicate that there is work to be done.

As the people congregate, as they join their bodies, minds, and spirits, the drumbeat loses its intensity and settles into a monotonous driving rhythm. As the drum leader, you are waiting, listening, building, and lowering the sacred sound according to the needs of the ceremony. As the drummer you are a servant, your place is powerful and therefore crucial, and you must be in synchronicity with the needs of the people and the ceremonial leaders. Wait for the feeling to change, to move, to stay, and to stop. Be ready for anything to happen.

If you are leading the drumming as well as the ceremony, which is most often the case, focus your drumming with your intention toward the vision of the ceremony, linking into and being directed by Spirit. When you are vocalizing a prayer, lower the volume of the drum so that you can be heard and the group can feel the words of the prayer. Between prayers, increase the drum volume, sending the prayer into its intended direction.

Go through the ceremony without interruption, letting others partake and be involved. However, as leader, take responsibility for the ceremony from beginning to end. When you have finished, privately and silently thank Spirit for letting you be the vehicle through which the ceremony happened.

This level of drumming is wonderful, whether you are the leader or as a member of the group.

It is all about listening, and staying in tune with others. Let go of any sense of self-importance, and sense your place in the overall picture.

Take your time to feel, watch, and wait.

left **Raise your drums to the sky, so that the light shines through the skins, to illuminate the beat and the feeling.**

If you enter a state of trance, open your faculties to learn from the experience, giving yourself totally to the flow.

Ceremonial drumming is very personal and you will have to find your own form of expression and connection through practice. It is especially useful to create your own ceremony on your own terms alone, so that your connection becomes deep and strong. When you are then given the opportunity to work in a larger group, you will be able to make an equal contribution to the whole, rather than waiting for someone else to always take the lead, and you will be firmly established in your contact with Spirit. Do not give away your power. Ceremony is like a river made up of lots of individual drops of water. No drop is more special or important than its neighbor. One drop might come from the spring source, whereas another could be a snowflake melting on a mountainside and another a raindrop falling from a summer shower. When they are all flowing in the river, they are all the same. Ceremonial drumming, too, flows like a river, the group consciousness tuning into the spiritual connection.

"Come, Great Spirit. Fill the hearts of your people, and kindle within us the fire of your love."

The drumming may be just for a short time, or it may go on for hours. It can be easy and euphoric or it can be difficult, tedious, and even painful.

The drummer goes with the feeling of the ceremonial needs. Feel the needs with your intuition, stretching yourself beyond your normal conscious boundaries, feeling for where you are needed.

Practice finding a steady beat on the drum.

Stay in your heart, do not get distracted by your ego.

A continuous rapid beat may lead you into a trance.

CREATING SACRED SPACE

Before you enter ceremony, you will need to detach yourself from the mundane world of eating, work, and family concerns. You bring your consciousness into focus through drumming the Sacred Directions and creating a space within which ceremony can happen. This is a protected zone in time and space; all of those people attending the ceremony need to be involved in this. Within this space, they become part of the group, almost initiated, and they will get a feeling of what this process is all about. This is a time of preparation, when those attending will be cleansed or smudged with sweet-smelling smoke of sage and frankincense. From the beginning of this setting-up of sacred space to the end of the ceremony, this whole piece of time and space needs to

be encapsulated in the protective energy of the four quarters, of the perpendicular axis of Mother Earth and Father Sky, and, most importantly, of the inner space of all those participating. Doubt and cynicism are very disturbing for a ceremony, so each person needs to feel at peace with themselves as well as with the other people there. This is the time of responding and clearing away resistance. This is not the time to prove to ourselves and others how important we are. We trust that Spirit will do the work when we set the process in motion; we "lift up the receiver and make the call." Spirit just needs us to be sincere and real about the whole event.

Start by setting up a Medicine Wheel using a colored stone or flag for each direction. This is going to be the physical zone within which the ceremony will happen. Invite someone to start drumming and ask them to stay focused on the function of the forthcoming ceremony. Put the stones in the center and then walk out in each direction, making a prayer to the spirit guardians of the directions, as well as to Grandmother Earth and Grandfather Sky (see page 30). Then stand silently and address *Wakan Tanka*, the power within you and all life. Once you have established your connection with the source, you can now take other stones and fill in the spaces between each quadrant, two between each compass point, making a total of twelve stones in all.

left The more we move to the light, the more the shadow reveals itself. Cleansing our space with sweet-smelling sage and frankincense is essential.

Now take the smudge stick or burning charcoal covered with herbs and your eagle feather and walk around the whole Medicine Wheel, making a prayer of cleansing and renewal. You are doing this as a vehicle for Spirit, so just walk around and around until you feel the space is clear. When sacred space has been created, the ceremony can naturally have a beginning.

"It was during the second world or the first ice age that all the five races of the children of Earth connected through the drum to the heartbeat of Earth Mother. They learned that the mother was active in their ceremonies and that amid the drumbeats

above In nature, we find our sacredness, and pray as a family. Our family grows as we understand how to invite all members.

there was a common, almost imperceptible rhythm seeming to emanate from the Earth. Whether in a cave or in the open of the forest, Earth's heartbeat would attune their heartbeats one to another"—Jamie Sams, *Sacred Path Cards*.

We can learn through the drumbeat to listen to the rhythm that connects us all, like a web without a weaver.

SACRED FIRE

The sacred fire and the drum are as closely entwined as the beat of the heart and the vitality of life. Fire is a sacred element from the earliest times. Prior to the first ice age, human beings depended on the warmth of the sun. As the first great ice age came, the two-leggeds found, out of necessity, how to harness the power of fire. This became central to the development of tribes and races. Fire kept us warm, and fire protected us from wild beasts and imaginary fears in the night. Fire cooked food and sharpened spears. Fire became the focus for social gatherings, dancing, and drumming. Around the fire, the stories of the hunt were re-enacted and the tribal legends created. The fire became the central theme for many sacred ceremonies. It brought people together in a circle, like the wheel of life, letting the community pray, celebrate, and hold ceremony around the tribal heart that blazed like the sun.

above **The fire of the sun warms and makes us grow. When we light a fire, we draw this fire out from the earth into ourselves.**

MAKING A SACRED FIRE

Make a fire with care and intention. See that it represents your ability to love and to be loved. Let it ignite your passion for life, spontaneity, and warmth. Clear a piece of land so that you have a circle of bare soil of at least 2 yards (about 2 meters) in diameter. Collect four large stones and set these up to mark the four directions and the fire's boundary and fill in the spaces with smaller stones to create a circle of stones. In the center, place a piece of wood for each of the Sacred Directions. Begin in the east, where light is born each day. Now build a platform made of wood.

On this platform, build a pyramid of small twigs, paper, and dry kindling. Light the paper and as the fire catches, slowly add the larger pieces of wood. Do not put on the biggest pieces of wood and logs until you have built up a strong foundation, which is burning well.

Build your logs on top of this burning fire. Imagine that each log is a piece of condensed sunlight. Ignite the fire as you seek to ignite your physical fire and watch it start from just a flicker, just a small bit of energy, and then develop into a blaze that demands respect; this fire represents your potential. Now you can start to develop the relationship between you, your drum, and the fire that you have built.

The center of our Grandmother Earth is full of fire. The oceans and land masses float over her molten depths like postal stamps on the surface of a balloon. Her hot fluid center circulates, boils, and bubbles, rising to the surface, then cooling and sinking down.

When we light a fire, we are drawing up this power out of the belly of our mother. Fire is a gift from our mother. As you begin your fire preparation, visualize this gift being drawn up from under her luxurious mantle.

When you light the fire, feel for the connection between the match, tinder, and twigs, and the rising fire flaming up to meet your intention. As larger pieces of wood and logs are placed on top, see this hole of fire becoming stronger and greater in size so that a tube of fire is blazing not only on the surface of the ground but symbolically down into the heart of the earth. Link the fire in your heart through the fire's heart into a warm love for the heart of the Earth Mother.

below Grandfather Sky is making love with our Grandmother Earth. Thunder beings are wondrous spirits born in the flash of lightning.

THE ELEMENTS

Earth, water, fire, and air are the four clan chiefs of the Earth Mother's world. These elements regulate the weather and the composition of space, energy, matter, and time. The elements are the basic building blocks of all creation and their structures interchange and are co-creative. In ceremony, the elements are brought together, their value and balance are renewed and honored.

The place of us humans relative to the elements is explored and put in perspective so that all who take part can feel the privilege of having a body to live in. This body is a temple held together physically, emotionally, intellectually, and spiritually by the elements. We are made out of particles of earth created from the food we eat and the water we drink. When we "change form," our tissues go back to those basic elements that started everything. We are made up of 70 percent water, which is two gases, hydrogen and oxygen, magically combined together, and in every particle of our being, the fire is unzipping the matter into energy and zipping it up from energy into matter elsewhere.

Water and earth have a mutual relationship as the foundation within which life can grow. Water shapes earth with the pounding ocean waves, drenching rains, and coursing rivers. In return, the Earth element recycles and facilitates the movement of water, letting it flow over itself, cleansing and releasing stagnation.

Air feeds fire. Without air, fire has nothing to rise up through, and air contains oxygen, one of the active ingredients on which fire feeds. Fire, as the warmth of the sun on the oceans and land, moves air in return, letting currents and winds flow. Fire and water are opposites: fire rises, warms, and activates; water falls, cools, and sedates.

Take one of each of the elements and place them, one in each quarter of the Medicine Wheel. Which one do you feel suits which direction? South corresponds to earth. Here we have growth, abundance, trees, plants, and children, the products and gifts of our Mother Earth. Your drum is made from her animal skins and hollow trees. So place in the south quadrant a living plant and some earth to signify your connection to this element.

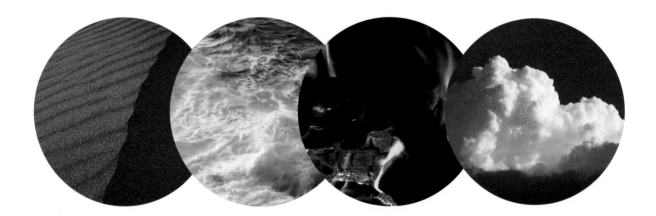

left The Medicine Wheel is a doorway to Spirit. Through this doorway, we can learn to be authentic.

bottom left Each of the Sacred Directions corresponds closely to one of the elements—air, earth, fire, and water.

The south winds are warm, full, and balmy, bringing easy-going and abundant feelings to all earth children.

West corresponds to water. Here we have cleansing— is there an element that can cleanse more effectively than water? Place a glass of pure spring water in the west and feel how dependent we all are on our Mother Earth's blood. The west wind brings rain and storms, and these winds, like water, have a powerful connection to the Moon Goddess. West winds bring the rain and is closely connected to the lunar and equinox cycles.

North corresponds to the element air. In the cool of winter, the air is close to the ground, and is drawn down to touch the earth. This is the aspect of non-substance and Spirit, where substance returns to the gaseous state, to await being made into physical form. Make smoke with incense or smudge to show the rising, white nature of air. North winds are cutting and biting. They penetrate deep into the tissues, telling you to close down, slow down, and wait for the fire of spring to return.

East corresponds to fire. Here is spring warmth and a rising sun to lighten and warm our winter and night-bound souls. The heart opens and rejoices in the face of the heat of the fire and its licking flames, the tissues open up and begin to shake free. Light a candle or a fire and feel how much more fire we all need.

"Come, Great Spirit, fill the Hearts of your people.
Enkindle within us the fire of your love.
Send forth your Spirit that we may be created
And thou shalt renew the face of your Earth."

Sit in the center of the Medicine Wheel. Facing each direction in turn. Then begin to beat your drum and see how you and these elements are related. Think about which ones really mean something to you, and or come out more during your drumming. Discover for yourself air and earth, earth and fire, and water and air, or any other combination of these elemental relationships.

MARKING TIME

"The holding of one's crystal or wotai *stone to the dawn, and recognizing that new knowledge can result from each new day, is a form of ceremony. Turning to the South at midday and recognizing that energy, health, growth, and shelter result from the Sun's warmth and light is a version of ceremony. Be sincere."*

ED MCGAA EAGLE MAN,
MOTHER EARTH SPIRITUALITY

Sunrise, sunset, solstice, equinox, celebrating the ancestors, and keeping a watch on the night—these are all times of celebration. As we relax in our lives and enjoy what is coming, our fears drop away since we have no more need of carrying them.

We must make time to mark time. Even dying, which is only one form changing into another form, is a celebration. So we take courage whenever we are to come out with our drums. We mark time when we can feel it is right to do so. We are part of a huge coordination, coming from Spirit, and the drums are like the voice. Something special happens when the drum is heard.

below left The temple of Stonehenge. Our solar system is carved into the geography of southern Britain, with the hub of the wheel at Stonehenge.

right When we connect with the pulse of nature, we get in tune with the source of life energy. We bring our spirit into alignment with the whole.

It is as if Mother Earth hears the drum and the voice. The spirit of nature responds to our developing connection. Each day is special. We mark the dawn with the sun coming up, especially on solstice and equinox, and find a special place to do so. Go someplace special, where you can relax and be yourself, and where you will not create a disturbance. Go to a hill or wood, near a waterfall, or in a glen. This is a sacred *wakan* opportunity to mark time. When we drum at these major turning points, at dawn and sunset, we know that over the surface of the planet there are others joining us.

"When you pray with that drum, when the spirits hear that drum, it echoes. They hear this drum, and they hear your voice loud and clear. It's like amplified. Like you get on the microphone, and it amplifies throughout the whole canyon. So the spirit could hear you. They could recognize your voice also. So when you're praying with that drum, your voice is amplified (via the drumming), and spirit can hear you."

WALLACE BLACK ELK,
THE SACRED WAYS OF A LAKOTA

A SOLSTICE SUNRISE

Go to your special place some time before you wish to begin the ceremony. Set up a sacred space with a central altar and place stones or flags in each quarter. As the sky becomes light, stand in a circle. Begin sounding and cleansing the chakras by chanting sacred sounds, such as om, into the earth and then into your base chakra, which is red. Move up through the body, going through each chakra and raising the sound as you progress upward. Stay together in sound. When everyone has finished call in through prayer all the guardians and angels. Visualize the crystal fire of the Earth Mother pouring up through the circle into everyone's hearts, and then call down the clear golden light of Grandfather Sky. As the sun rises, feel the two lights merge in the heart area, and visualize a pink rose in the center of the group. Send the power of the new dawn, mixed with your combined love, down the line of the rising light, toward other celebrators. Drum as you go, but while people pray aloud, let the drums be gentle so that their prayers can be felt and heard. Gradually build up the drum sound, sending the prayers out to Spirit and into the world.

CLEANSING

We need to be clean in mind, body, and spirit. Washing with hot water and soap, and covering ourselves with sweet-smelling odors, is not enough. We need to appreciate that the movement of water in the cooling rains, streams, rivers, and oceans is a majestic cycle of cleansing. When we wash ourselves, we are taking part in a cleansing ritual that is an ancient relationship between the land dwellers and the sea. We return for a short while to the womb, connecting ourselves through contact with water to the Great Mother. Have respect for water, for it is the greatest of all cleansers.

Before the ceremony, wash in clear, fresh, and cold water: your face, hands, and hair, crystals and stones, working tools, dishes, and bowls. For ceremonial work, it

"My heart is filled with joy when I see you here,
As the brooks fill with water
when the snows melt in the spring.
And I feel glad as the ponies do
when the fresh grass starts
in the beginning of the year. "

TEN BEARS, *TOUCH THE EARTH*

is essential that the sacred space, the instruments, and the people taking part are cleansed. We all have our own agenda, our own history and pain, and we can often come to a ceremony cynical and suspicious. This will get in the way of other participants' sincerity and their need for touching the natural reality, which ceremony awakens. So, as much as possible, everyone needs to be equal with each other and come into ceremony open-minded. We all go through the same form of cleansing as we enter the site, which itself has been made sacred with prayer and smoke from sweet-smelling herbs. Each herb carries its own power and healing properties; when burned, their smoke clears the atmosphere of negative vibrations.

left **I cleanse my body each day, but my spirit also needs cleansing. We do this as a team so that we all benefit and we all stay clear.**

right Eagle and hawk feathers are used to clear the auras of people coming for healing.

HERBS FOR SMUDGING

Sagebrush, as used in smudge sticks, is native to the United States. This herb is very cleansing; it transforms energy and brings change.

Sage, as used in cooking, brings healing and wisdom, and is effective for increasing spiritual awareness.

Sweetgrass attracts positive energy.

Lavender is a herb that restores balance and creates a peaceful atmosphere.

Rosemary brings clarity, is a powerful healer, and assists in taking in new experiences.

Mugwort cleanses away women's health problems. This herb is very warming, and stimulates psychic awareness and prophetic dreams.

Juniper creates a safe and sacred space.

Cedar is especially useful for clearing negative emotion and healing. This herb is also deeply purifying.

Frankincense clears away evil spirits and removes fear.

With the tongs, hold your charcoal over a candle or naked flame. When it is burning, place it into the shell or bowl. Let it get really hot and then put on one or more of the cleansing herbs. Take up the feather or bird's wing and use it to push the smoke into the air. If you are using a smudge stick, light it thoroughly, then blow out any flames, and either waft the smoke with the feather or move the stick around and around in circles in the area to be cleansed. Always ensure that after the cleansing the charcoal and the smudge stick are extinguished.

"Sweetgrass invokes positive and negative spirits. Cedar, which is used to bless the hot rocks as they enter the sweat lodge, and in the loading of the Sacred Pipe. Sage which chases negative spirits away."

CHIEF ARCHIE FIRE LAME DEER,
THE LAKOTA SWEAT LODGE CARDS

DRUMMING THE SACRED DIRECTIONS

*"When people live far from the scenes
of the Great Spirit's making,
it's easy for them to forget his laws."*

WALKING BUFFALO,
TOUCH THE EARTH

The Sacred Directions ceremony is the foundation of Native American spirituality. It is based on the fact that each one of us stands in the center of our own life experience, choosing our future based on our past experience, and yet living and breathing in the reality of now. The Sacred Directions are measured from your position in the universe as the four points of the compass—south, *itokaga*; west, *wiyopeyata*; north, *waziya*; and east, *wiyoheyapa*; forming a cross with you at the center. The two aspects down toward the earth are *ina maka*, below your feet, and *makpiyahate*, up into the sky above your head; the last direction is inside, into your inner universe.

Track 1 on the CD gives you an opportunity to pray to the Sacred Directions. The ceremony starts with intention. A colored stone is set in each of the cardinal directions. Stand in the center and "be" centered. Trust in the feeling and have confidence in yourself. If there are more people taking part, then stand outside the circle of stones and face each direction in turn. As you listen to the track,

you will hear the tune hummed gently, introduced by the melody played on a flute.

Face south and sing: *"Spirit of the south, spirit of the south, bring me healing and laughter."* In the drumming interval, make your prayers to the power of the south. *"I call on the power of the south, the spirit of healing, the plants, flowers, and healing herbs. I call upon the spirit of laughter, joy, and children. I call the spirit of summer, the full heat of midday and abundance. I am grateful for this vision of wholeness, I am grateful for all that is given to me."*

When you hear the flute, turn clockwise to the west and sing your prayers to the west on the humming tune: *"Spirit of the west, spirit of the west, bring me cleansing and insight."* As before, in the drumming interval, make your prayers to the west. *"I call on the spirit of the west, the spirit of prayer, the spirit of introspection, of going inside and facing myself in prayer, cleansing, and meditation. I call on the spirit of the rain and the moist west winds to help me face my own shadow and wash away my fear of darkness. I call the grandfathers and grandmothers and all those who have gone before us. I am grateful for all that is given to me."*

Turn clockwise to the north and sing: *"Spirit of the north, spirit of the north, bring me wisdom and purity."* As before, in the drumming interval, turn and make your prayers to the north. *"I call on the spirit of the north, the journey into old age, to the spirit of wisdom and purity. I call on the Great Mother, White Buffalo Calf Woman. I call on the spirit of contraction, scarcity, and winter, which teaches me to be humble before the natural cycles of which I am part. I call on the angels and spirit guides to protect me on this earth walk. I am grateful for all that is taken from me."*

above Cherish your beautifully painted drum and use it with intent when carrying out any ceremony.

right Seek the spirits of the Sacred Directions with your drum saying, "Calling, I hear myself calling you. Falling, I don't want to fall away."

Turn to face the east and sing: "*Spirit of the east, spirit of the east, help the new dawn in me rising.*" As before, in the drumming interval, turn and make your prayers to the east. "*I call to the east, to the place of new beginnings, where the sun rises, and spring bursts forth, where life is conceived within life, to be born as future generations. I call to the spirit of the living masters, all those living who inspire us with their lives. Spirit, show us how to be ready for anything. I am grateful for the fresh and the new.*"

Touch the earth with the drum and sing: "*Grandmother Earth, Grandmother Earth, you give me food and shelter.*" As before, in the drumming interval, make your prayers. "*Mother Earth, I thank you for this physical body that you give me to shelter my spirit. I thank you for my wife/husband, children, family, and friends. I thank you for all the food and clothing that I use. It comes from you; I am grateful. Mother Earth, help me learn to give to you as you constantly give to me. I am grateful for all that is given to me.*"

Reach your hands and drum up towards the sky and sing: "*Grandfather Sky, Grandfather Sky, you breathe the breath of life into me.*" As before, in the drumming interval, make your prayers. "*Grandfather Sky, I thank you for this gift of prayer, and for the breath that breathes me. You pour forth your warmth from the sun that heats the land and oceans, creating the cycles, giving plants and animals the energy to live. How can I ever find the words to thank you? I am grateful for my life.*"

Go inside yourself and sing: "*Spirit of Within, Spirit of Within, you are my appreciation.*" As before, in the drumming interval, make your prayers. "*To that which looks out and appreciates and hears from within beautiful sounds. To that part of me inside that reaches into the source of the breath that is so sweet to taste. Spirit, I am grateful to be part of you.*"

There is then a long piece of drumming on the CD, during which you can make additional prayers if you feel that there is something that needs your attention.

CLEARING AND CLEANSING SPACE WITH THE DRUM

There are three main aspects of cleansing and clearing space using your drum.

INNER CLEARING BEFORE CEREMONY

This work is wonderful, for you will get to spend quality time on your own, in your sacred space inside the house or in nature, doing something that you will find increasingly valuable—staying clear. It becomes a form of channeling the spirit. You pick up your drum, find your beat, connect to Spirit—and Spirit is with you. Especially when you know that you have an important issue to deal with, make sure that you spend time getting yourself linked to that which is going to support you: your spirit guides in the north, your living teachers in the east, the spirits of the herbs in the south, and your ancestors in the west.

Make this time special for you, and eat a light meal beforehand. Have a wash or bath, drink lots of water, smudge yourself with cleansing herbs and then link yourself to source through meditation.

Be humble and ask for help as you drum gently to yourself. I often just quietly pad the skin with my hand, listening and waiting for inspiration. You will know when you are ready to start clearing and cleansing space.

left "Great Spirit, help me
to connect to you. You will be
the voice speaking through
me, you are the silent
whisper in my heart."

"The Drum is the Great Spirit's favorite instrument. That's why we were all given a heartbeat."

MANO, NAVAJO ELDER

DRUMMING OUT THE GHOSTS

Going around a house or dwelling with the drum, clearing through all the rooms and corners, drumming out all the negative spirit energy that has been collecting there, is a wonderful service that you can give to your family and friends. Often these energies are not harmful, but it is always better to live in a space that is neutral and clear from the past. Be intuitive with your drumming. In some areas it needs to be gentle and the drum does not seem to say much. Then, all of a sudden, you really need to hit the drum, as if there is something that needs to be shifted. Learn to follow your intuition.

Prepare by praying to the Sacred Directions and smudging yourself. Keep calling on the presence of your spirit guides and ancestors to protect you. Do it with lighthearted seriousness. Some of the energies you will encounter are sticky and horrible. You do not want to take them home with you, yet you do not need to be too serious—know

above **This drum will manifest the power of the bear, being strong and direct. This is strong medicine for clearing space.**

that Spirit is there to protect you. When you have finished, smudge yourself again and wash in fresh water. Then spend some time on your own, meditating and expressing your gratitude to the spirit world for its help.

CLEARING ANOTHER PERSON'S AURA

It is important to be well prepared. Give yourself the quality time as described for Drumming the Sacred Directions. If you are not prepared for a situation, call on Spirit, go through the Sacred Directions silently inside yourself, and watch yourself becoming connected. When clearing someone's aura with the drum, quickly find out their basic need, and have them face the appropriate direction. They should face South if they need healing, West if they need cleansing or connecting to the ancestors, North if they are seeking inner wisdom, and East if they are looking for a new direction.

Stand facing each other, honoring each other's presence. Drum around them about 3¼ yards (3 meters) away from their physical body, using your own beat. Do not try to discover their personal sound; this is something that is experienced in healing and medicine drumming. Go up and down over the body, feeling for obstructions in their energy field. If you feel resistance, let the drumming become more forceful, pushing away that resistance with the beat. When you have finished, cleanse yourself and give thanks to Spirit.

You can use track 2 on the CD for space clearing. Generally, this type of drumming has more variety and flare. The drums start gently, but the volume and the beat increases where there is an obstruction or stagnation.

MEDICINE AND HEALING
WITH THE SACRED DRUM

*"The most important law in medicine
is absent from every medical text book,
and that is that the difference between
dead tissue and live tissue is that living tissue heals itself."*

DR MICHAEL ASH

This medicine has the power of the earth and heaven and the Sacred Directions. It dives into and encompasses the very depths of human disease, to a level that we in the sophisticated modern world cannot behold in our wildest dreams. We have to unlearn the conditioning we have learned, drop our fear, and stop our attack on the organisms that make up 90 percent of our body cells. Native medicine not only sees us as part of our environment, but as our environment.

By vocation, I am a physician of natural medicine, and since I was a child, I have experienced the wonders of healing through prayer, healing touch, tools, herbs, and trust. Medicine and healing with the drum is exciting because it requires such a high level of intuition and total surrender. Ego and self-importance get in the way, so be prepared to let them go. Before you do a healing ceremony, prepare yourself as previously described in the section on Drumming the Sacred Directions.

Smudge the person who is asking for help with sage, lavender, or cedar. Make prayers strong for their healing.

Sit that person down, facing the direction that is right for the healing. Ask what they want, and Spirit will come.

Place a colored stone on the ground for each of the directions and go through the Sacred Directions within yourself, creating a bubble of safety.

Ask for absence of empty conversation.

When you feel ready, start the healing ceremony.

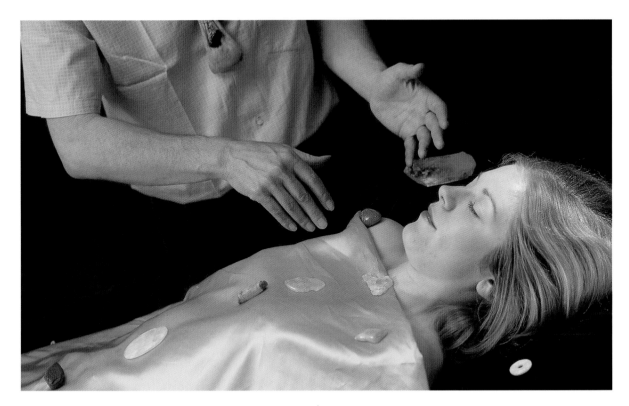

Begin drumming around the person asking for healing, 6–9 feet (2–3 meters) away from them, and search to find their beat. There is no hurry; stay focused on being a vehicle for Spirit. Your safest place is to stay inside, keeping a watch out and staying empty of your own judgments. Every human being and their growth is very precious, so you need to be sensitive. As you move around, you will find areas where the drum seems to sing, and the sound is absolutely beautiful. You may even find yourself singing a song that is coming out of the air—this is a gift for you to observe and for the person sitting there to receive. It is just coming through you, so let it go as it has come and do not try to remember it. In other areas and at other times the drum seems to get very strong, as if the sound is pushing away an obstruction. Like a road that is jammed, this can be cleared by the drumbeat, so go with it for as long as it lasts. There is also a time when the energy stops, so follow that feeling when it happens.

Fade the drumming out slowly and let the receiver of this experience find their way back securely. Put the drum down and place your hands on their shoulders. Sit down in front of them, looking down or eyes closed. Hold their feet or hands. Make contact that says the ceremony is over, yet be very sensitive.

Track 3 of the CD features drumming for medicine and healing. This has a similar feel to clearing and cleansing, but this is personal medicine for the receiver. On this track, the changes of rhythm and beat flow along with 2–4 drums and a rattle.

above Healing is the power of God coming through our hands, eyes, and actions. Without pure intention, our tools are useless.

far left The sweet smoke clears thought forms clinging to our spirit. Our thoughts create our reality; we must keep our thoughts clear.

MEDICINE LODGES AND HEALING CIRCLES

All over this modern world, more and more people are seeking a greater connection to real spirituality. They feel as if they have a part to play in this incredible time of earth changes. These people have felt impotent about what they can do at this volatile time. As they become more open, they know that Mother Earth needs us to co-operate and use our healing gifts rather than destroy her beauty with our carelessness. Modern society is not really in touch with the needs of this beautiful planet. It is only the people of indigenous cultures who have continued their tradition of respecting and caring for the earth, because they have been taught for hundreds of years that the beauty and health of the Earth, and her influence on our physical, mental, emotional, and spiritual well-being, cannot be replaced.

Healing circles and medicine lodges are a practical and spiritual answer to this. Practically, they bring people of similar interests together, so that communication about what is really happening at a global level can be shared

"Healthy feet can hear the very heart of Holy Earth."

SITTING BULL,
TOUCH THE EARTH

below left When I enter the stone people lodge, I put my head on the earth and say, "to all my relations."

right When we let go of our self-importance and enter the circle, Great Spirit laughs with us.

and discussed. This is not a time for doom-watching, and no political agendas are proposed within the circle.

The drumbeats gently invite those present to form a circle. They come together as a group to draw the energy of the Sacred Directions into the hoop. They begin to vision light being drawn down from the heavens and the healing power of the earth being drawn up to meet in our hearts. These are blended with the powers of north, east, south, and west to create a vortex of powerful intent. The circle is stirred sunwise, bringing in all that may be of assistance. As the energy rises, the prayers become stronger and deeper. The drum beats, bringing everyone into the same breathing pattern, bringing everyone together as one. When the charge of spiritual desire is brimming and ready to flow out, the energy is distributed toward countries, societies, individuals' health and happiness, and anything that needs healing.

Within this sacred space, people then break off into groups to receive or give healing. Sometimes this happens in a group setting, with more than one person receiving healing and more than one person giving.

These medicine lodges or healing circles are both a wonderful opportunity and a great inspiration.

Gather together a group of people with a similar spiritual path to you as part of the healing circle.

Start the evening with everyone being smudged.

Drum through the Sacred Directions and perform a clearing space ceremony.

Explain to newcomers what they might expect to see and hear as part of a healing circle.

Go around the group in a clockwise direction, inviting each person in turn to sit in the middle of the circle to receive healing. Let others in the circle find their place as instruments of the great Spirit's love.

Someone may get up to stand behind the person in the center and place their hands on the shoulders, with someone else at the feet, and someone else holding the hands.

Drum, rattle, song, and chanting can happen.

You set up the atmosphere with your intention and you keep the highest level of awareness throughout the healing. Go with the flow—stop only when the energy leaves your circle and the people within it.

When one person is finished, invite another to sit in the center. Some only want to give; they too can receive.

At the end, when there is no one left to receive healing, close the evening with a prayer of gratitude to the spirits and ask each person to wash their hands before they start conversations about their personal experiences.

MEDITATING WITH THE DRUM

"Every so often the Heart says, 'Fill me'
And this can cause great anguish
if you don't know how.
To me, the priority must be to listen.
To listen to what the heart has to say.
To listen to what this voice has to say to me."

MAHARAJI, *REFLECTIONS*

Meditation is the process of going inside ourselves and making contact with the source. Our source is the same for each one of us—a continuous flow of life that starts somewhere deep inside this human temple and bubbles up through our senses. With the drum, we can go deep into the place of stillness and listen for what the heart has to say.

Start the meditation process by finding a quiet spot where you will not be disturbed.

If you are inside a house with other people around, use your hand instead of the drumstick so that you do not attract unnecessary attention to your meditation. Gently begin your drumming.

Find your beat, watch, and listen. Enjoy all the little sounds that come through your drum.

Feel the contact between the body of your drum and your own body. Let yourself feel at one with the sound.

Relax and take some deep breaths; let the resonance of the drum and your breath come together.

As you go into this experience of uniting the drumbeat with your own internal rhythms, let the drumming slow down as you look for your heartbeat.

Halve the drumbeat so that the rhythm becomes easy yet slower than before.

Let go of your focus on the drum; stay looking and listening inside. What do you see? What do you hear? What do you feel? Let yourself go deeper, into the beat. Do not worry if the drumming stops; stay focused on your inner experience. If you become distracted and you need to get back into meditating, just focus on the drumbeat again. When the time comes for you to stop meditating, bring yourself back by drumming a steady beat.

A DRUMMING MEDITATION

In group meditations, the drum is a wonderful tool for holding the space and keeping the participants in focus. This is a relaxing and therefore gentle process to be handled with sensitivity and clear intent.

Set up a Medicine Wheel in the center of the circle. Light a smudge stick and cleanse the space. Each person in the circle needs to be spiritually washed with smoke. Explain to the participants the reason for the meditation and what is expected.

Start drumming; there can be more than one person drumming. Encourage people to join in beforehand.

Gently feel and direct the beat of the drum so that a feeling of peace fills the whole room.

Intuitively connect with each person, establishing a common bond of focus in the group.

Ensure that each drummer is connected to the beat.

Invite each person to synchronize their breathing, so that you all breathe in and out together.

Link the drumbeat to the common breath.

Quiet the drum so that the beat is like a heartbeat holding the space. Stay clear in your intention.

Quiet the sound even more so that it is hardly audible.

Keep a steady beat, but lift the volume at times to bring people back when they lose focus.

Hold the meditation for 30 minutes.

When you feel that it is time to bring the people back out of the meditation, increase the volume of the drum and break up the drumbeat.

Drum for a while, allowing no conversation, enabling each person to feel grounded.

left Go inside yourself as if you are a student, learning to be authentic, learning to find your rhythm, your connection to life.

Explore track 4 of the CD to meditate with the drum. This is a long and very gentle drum session, which is a wonderful opportunity for the novice to overlay sound upon a solid warm beat. It is also a wonderful opportunity for meditation.

"And you will know when you are filled. You have the capacity to know if you allow yourself. Drink the water. When your thirst is quenched, you will know. You will feel."
MAHARAJI, *REFLECTIONS*

"The breath is the common drum upon which all life beats."
MICHAEL GREAT MOUNTAIN ASH

DRUMMING AND PRAYER

> *"Tribal peoples all over the planet still rely upon the drum to connect the energy of each person participating in ritual, prayer, or ceremony."*
>
> **JAMIE SAMS,** *SACRED PATH CARDS*

The energy, focus, and, above all, the heightened consciousness of the people present in a drumming group is drawn together and can be directed toward healing, prayer, and gratitude. This is often a more powerful way to pray and direct the feelings and prayers that you want to project out to different people. This collective consciousness is anchored by the drum and links the heart pulse of the holy earth to the hearts of the individuals, leaving no room for manipulation and hysteria. It is most important that the prayer is directly linked to Spirit and that it is selfless. We must learn to serve this power that fills us with each breath of life. When we pray as individuals or in the collective, we create through it a light center, where angels, sacred ancestors, personal guides, and all holy beings are welcome. The more we pray, call, drum, and invoke the spirit, the more we become part of the healing of the planet. Each of us is a reflection of the whole, and the whole blesses us for our attitude, courage, and example.

DRUMMING AND PRAYING

First, understand clearly why you are praying. When you are ready, start the drumming. Create a sacred space and smudge all those present.

Feel comfortable with silence, and then start to pray aloud when you feel the power is coming through you.

As you pray, call in the collective energy of the group so that you are all focused on the same outcome.

If others want to make a prayer, invite them to do so. You do not have to pray for too long. Spirit prefers swift, direct prayer, so feel for the time to stop.

When you are ready to stop, emphasize the qualities of trust and gratitude, because it is the collective faith and hope that calls Spirit to answer our prayers.

AN ACTIVE DRUM AND PRAYER MEDITATION FOR WORLD PEACE

Invite those who are present to gather in a circle around the Medicine Wheel. Smudge each of the participants and the room. Explain the process involved and what is expected of everyone; you may want them to put in their own prayers at the end, or you may ask them to hold hands at a certain time. Let people know beforehand so that it is not a surprise for them when something such as this happens within the ceremony.

Begin drumming and tune the sound to the intention of the meditation—in this case, it is for world peace. Invite the presence of each of the Sacred Directions into the circle, creating a safe and powerful space.

Begin to stretch the focus of the circle into peace toward each person's family.

Put the intention into the community. Stretch the peace of the circle into the state, and the country as a whole.

Stretch the peace still more until the whole globe is surrounded with the intended peace.

Where you feel there is special need—for instance, in the Balkans, Middle East, or Tibet—increase the drumbeat for a few minutes, using the sound as a route for the global healing energy.

Let the drum rhythm change and fluctuate according to the circumstance and feeling in the space.

When you have finished, bring the energy back into the circle for a minute or two.

Thank the spirits of the Sacred Directions, this time in an antisunwise direction. Above, below, south, west, north, east, and within. This unwinds the energy and brings the people back to where they started.

Pass your talking stick sunwise around the circle and invite everyone to discuss their experiences.

THE TALKING STICK

The talking stick is traditionally made from a piece of wood that has special significance for its keeper. It can be carved and decorated with stones, crystals, feathers, and colored leather or string. A leather pouch, containing sacred objects, can be tied to the stick to add to its power. After ceremony or group healings and meditations, the talking stick is handed from person to person around the circle. You can share your experience when you are holding the stick; if not, you have to wait your turn.

Using the talking stick is good for family discussions and arguments because it creates a structure where everyone has the opportunity to share their views and opinions. The talking stick is a stick of truth, and you must speak only the truth when you are holding it.

above Umbilical cords and the first teeth of my children, hair from my mother and my wife, the birchwood chewed by a beaver—the talking stick has power.

background picture In the wilderness, we can pray, away from all the distractions of our everyday lives.

TRANCE DRUMMING

"We need to adjust our nature and habits to synchronize our vibrational rate with the power. This is the purpose of Shamanic drumming."

KENNETH MEADOWS,
SHAMANIC EXPERIENCE

Trance drumming is very powerful, but make sure that you are well prepared and do it with people who are experienced in doing it. You are carried into the trance with either a rattle or drum, and the beat is fast, between 200 and 210 beats per minute (according to Belinda Gore in *Ecstatic Body Postures*) or between 160 to 220 beats per minute (according to Kenneth Meadows in *Shamanic Experience*).

It is a rapid continuous beat with no counterbeats or cross rhythms. The flowing beat of the drum modifies the rate of vibration within all levels of the energetics of our being, enabling our consciousness to entwine with the flow of spirit energy. You lose the concept of time, moving into the *nagual*, or stream of universal consciousness within the life force. The drumming brings you safely back into present time when the trance is over. It acts like an anchor, as does fire, and lets the spirit feel safe, exploring beyond its normal physical confines. Have no expectations, since you may be disappointed. During the trance you may "journey" and yet you will be aware of your physical body. The change is subtle, and one in which your willingness to be open to see and be spoken to by Spirit seems to come alive. You can talk and walk with Spirit in a heightened awareness, letting fly areas that are usually grounded.

It is good to get to know that everyone can experience trance, and you can let yourself enter this state as often as you feel the need. Go in with a sincere heart to seek guidance for selfless reasons.

"I have no plan. I have no power;
But when we pray, the spirit came
and suggested that.
But we never know what they
are going to do."

WALLACE BLACK ELK,
THE SACRED WAYS OF A LAKOTA

Go through the Sacred Directions ceremony, praying for a safe and fruitful trance experience. Call in the presence of your spirit guides by name and request that they stay with you throughout the timeless period.

Either lie in the "South American Lower World Posture"—on your back with your left arm covering your eyes; or sit crossed-legged on the ground with your palms face down on your knees; or stand in the "Singing Shaman Posture"—with both hands gently clenched and positioned on the chest over the heart, so that the knuckles of the little fingers touch. Bend your knees slightly and lift your face to Grandfather Sky.

Let the drumming begin or start the tape. Place the stone in one of your hands, for this is your connection to the holy earth. Hold the posture and follow the sound of the drum or rattle. Let yourself be led through the sound and your breath to slow down. Be aware of the protective forces that bless you in this work and trust the direction in which you will be led. In the beginning, until you become more experienced, enter into each trance posture position for fifteen minutes only. End with prayers of gratitude and a sharing of your experiences using the talking stick. It is usual to give the drummer a small gift for being the anchor for your experience.

Trance drumming features on track 7 of the CD. This is a wonderful opportunity for both the novice and the experienced drummer to learn to keep a fast and even beat with drum and rattle. This is also an excellent example of trance drumming for someone to explore the experience of posture or medicine trances.

left **Find your crazy wild part, the part that needs to be released and free, the child, the warrior, the authentic self.**

DRUMMING UP THE SPIRITS

"This message is a message of hope. The Hopi and Maori Elders say that we are moving into this time, this time of the World of the Fifth Hoop. This is a time when all the four Sacred Powers are going to be reconnected."

**LARRY MERCULIEFF,
AT THE WISDOM-KEEPERS
OF THE NORTH CONFERENCE,
KINDRED SPIRIT MAGAZINE**

The spirit of a living being does not cease to exist when we die, in the same way that bluebells and daffodils do not die when they have finished blooming. Their spirit goes into another form and waits in the holy earth until they are called out again to be part of the never-ending cycle of life. It is the same with humans when they pass on to another form. You and I will "drop our robe" and what happens is part of the Great Mystery. As a society, we will always question this phenomenon. You, too, must question, and if you do so with the drum, you may find some answers.

The ancestors, or the spirits of those who have gone before us, are available to us and are as close to you as you wish them to be. They can be called upon to intercede and support our growth and spiritual development

through the drum. They can hear when we call. Drumming teaches us how to call. Traditionally the ancestors are in the West, where the sun goes down. The time of day to call to them is ideally in the black of night. In the spirit-calling ceremony of the Lakota, or *yuwipi*, the medicine person is bound into blankets and placed in the middle of the room in complete darkness.

Ensure that phones or visitors will not interrupt you. Create a sacred space with smudge and red (east), yellow (south), black (west), and white (north) stones. Call in your spirit guides and protective spirits. Smudge yourself and your helpers; as you do this, prepare your prayer or reason for calling on the ancestors.

Make sure the room is free of light, and face west to begin drumming. Let yourself speak out your prayer, and call on those on the other side of the veil who you know lived in truth and integrity. If for any reason you feel uncomfortable with the spiritual energy that has entered the room, call on the presence of your spirit guides, or Archangel Michael, the archetypal protective spirit guide, with his huge sword of truth. Trust what happens and know that you are constantly protected when you do this work—and nothing will go wrong. Keep it light and let the drumming keep you connected to the sacred earth throughout the ceremony.

In the North are the spirits of the angels, spirit guides, Mother Mary, White Buffalo Calf Woman. The north aspect is wonderful for drumming up the Spirits because your spirit is so safe. Prepare yourselves as with the West, and then call the specific spirits or guides that you feel can help you in your prayer. We call the spirits of the

North when we have needs with regard to our strength of will, endurance during hard times, and the need for clarity and wisdom.

Personally, I have found drumming in the south direction invaluable when working with the plant and tree spirits and collecting herbs and flowers for medicines. Place a gift of tobacco or a stone onto the ground by the plant you are seeking to know or use in medicine. With your eyes open, drum to the plant and speak or sing to it about its beauty; honor this living being as one of your relatives. Let your consciousness be drawn within the subtle energy of the plant, and on the physical side smell and "gaze" without focus toward the plant's physical appearance. If you are going to remove a part of the plant, do so with respect and a prayer, and put a drop of your saliva onto the exposed cut surface.

We drum to the east when we are seeking Spirit's guidance for new directions or new knowledge. The east is like sowing seeds, so when we call the spirits of the east, it is new beginnings that we are seeking. Spirit drumming in the other directions—south for healing, west for your ancestors, and north for your spirit guides—tends to be more powerful and energy building.

We have a lot to learn from the Native American Elders about spirit calling and I recommend you read Wallace Black Elk, Ed McGaa Eagle Man, John Fire, and Archie Fire Lame Deer to get more of an in-depth understanding (see bibliography).

above **With the pipe, White Buffalo Calf Woman came to the people. She sang, "On the visible breath I came walking, in a sacred manner I walk."**

GROUP DRUMMING

In this modern age, technology and our ability to cope with its constant improvement leads us and our young on a path of illusion that is trapping our spirits. Television and computers make for static bodies and hyperactive brains. We then absorb the information that we are fed and believe it to be true.

We all are seeking something deeper, where we can respond as a group and experience interaction, where we can converse without words and yet truly release our feelings. A place where we can feel a cooperation that connects us to the heart beating in the same time within each of our chests, and also connects us to the rhythm of the holy earth. The sound of drumming can penetrate the very bones of everyone, bringing us all together. Everyone can take part, from the old man steadily striking his ancient drum, to the little girl who has found two sticks and a pan. The drumming brings the generations together without the limitations of conversation. It is music to the human flesh, which loves to move in rhythm and sway in time. Our bodies need spontaneous laughter and the opportunity to sing, chant, and move, sometimes

> *"The signs of this time of healing*
> *that is to start are,*
> *When the children bring back*
> *the spirit of the village."*
>
> **LARRY MERCULIEFF,**
> ***TRIBAL VOICES***

shriek or bellow, like a wild animal. We need a safe space to express these needs, where we will not be judged as mad, but welcomed as being expressive.

"We can turn the directions and vision for truth,
From wisdom and death through conception and youth.
Our drums can start beating, they are timed to the pulse.
The heart can then tune so that life is not false.
We can all breathe together, breathing deeply as one
All life is booming on the breath as a drum."

To find a drumming group, go to your nearest shop that sells good-quality, hand-made drums and ask for contacts, or look in alternative living magazines for advertisements. You will soon find a drum leader, who will welcome you into their group.

Drumming groups are a way of creating a strong healing circle, where both men and women can feel equal benefit and opportunity to contribute. If you want to start your own group, start by speaking to people who drum (as many as possible) and invite them to meet up in your house for an evening "pow-wow." Do first warn your neighbors—if you get enough support, this can become a regular activity. It is also good to host a drumming group

The sea breathes in waves,
in tides, and in swells,
The land breathes in seasons,
in rainfall and smells."
BUFFALO SPIRIT MAN

far left Drumming has power;
as a people, we are powerful.
We can enter that power only
when we give ourselves
permission to drop our disguise.

below Moving around the circle
sunwise, we spin with the
energy of creation, co-creating
with heaven and earth, and everything to which we are related.

outside in natural surroundings and around a fire, which draws people into a circle. Outside in the open air drums have a special quality because the elements are so close. Air, fire, water, and earth can be touched by your spirit and the drummers can resonate with the vibrations of these forces that nature exudes. You will also feel much less self-conscious during the early days when you are learning if you drum in a group of experienced drummers. Group drumming is a wonderful way to release stress and tension. A level of communication begins to flow between the members. The overall result is the combination of the whole.

Track 5 on the CD features group drumming, and is a wonderful opportunity to let fly and really open up your drumming skills. This track includes drums and rattles.

DRUMMING AWAY FEAR, ANGER, AND SADNESS

"I think we are moving in a circle, or maybe a spiral, going a little higher every time, but still returning to the same point. We are moving closer to nature again. I feel it, you feel it too."

JOHN FIRE LAME DEER,
LAME DEER SIOUX MEDICINE MAN

The drum is a powerful tool for letting go of our feelings of anger, fear, and sadness. Part of this process of learning to walk the medicine path is to experience both the ups and the downs. Life is like the sea: the tide comes in when you take your first breath and the tide goes out when you take your last breath. The sun rises and we all warm up and run around, then the sun goes down and we have to cuddle up and stay warm. All life is circles within circles, and we are very much part of it.

Fear is the emotion that the majority of human disorders are based on. As Dr. Jampolsky says, "Love is letting go of fear." In Chinese medicine, fear is linked to the kidneys and bladder, to the bones, hearing, and sexuality. There are more points of healing for psychic disorders on the bladder energy meridian than on all the other meridians put together. The way to heal all fear diseases is to send love to the cause of the fear. With your drum, focus

below The drum's beat breaks
through the stagnation,
inducing change. Spirit comes
through the drum releasing
fear, anger, and sadness.

your attention on the source of your fear—or whatever
you can establish as the closest thing to its essence. Drum
into that place and pour into it all the sacred energy that
you can find. If you still feel fearful when you are finished,
have a break, then start the process again.

Anger is an emotion of the liver, where feelings need to
be expressed but have been repressed. You will need to let
out the frustration that cannot find an exit. Again, it is a
matter of timing. Let the drum bring you back into time
with the whole. Hold the drum, and send your prayer into
your source as you beat and with powerful intent ask to be
released from your false expectations. Ask through the
drum how to let the anger disperse.

Sadness is a sickness of the lungs. It is long and linger-
ing and forces us to hold onto the past. Sadness is white
and cold and needs the warmth of the rising sun in the
East to see that there is new growth, opportunity, and
experience coming as the constant wave of the present
keeps moving on and forward. Breathe with the drum and
find your drumbeat as close to the breath as possible.
Push the sound through the breath into the source and
ask to have the pain taken away. Sing this little song as you
drum, and make up your own tune: *"Please take the pain
away, please take the pain away. Please take the pain away,
please take the pain away."*

*"Earth Mother is trying to help us remove
the stuff we have stuck in our bodies,
inherited from the spiritual sickness
of generations and generations."*

LARRY MERCULIEFF,
A WISDOM-KEEPER OF THE NORTH

DRUMMING FOR WOMEN

For the past 4,000 years the energetic dominance of the world has been stuck in the male side, in thinking from the brain and managing life attitudes from the top downward: "I think therefore I am." This attitude does not allow for intuition and feelings from the heart and tends to be aggressive. The process of life is pushed forward by an individual rather than from the family or community and leading by an example that is connected to the natural way. It is not a bad energy, but it has become out of balance with the feminine force, which is totally different in nature. Female energy is healing, nurturing, sharing, and caring. It contains feeling, loving, and touching, and places the family as the unit of the community rather than the individual.

All of us have both male and female sides, the yin and yang energies that complement and contrast with each other. Our true nature has no gender, name, nor nationality, but we are born female or male to learn the lessons that our soul needs to learn.

The circle, where all are equal, is the symbol for the feminine energy. The ego is a male characteristic and although a necessary part of our desire to grow and move forward, it is held in control and kept in balance by the group consciousness, which is female in nature. The world's spiritual leaders today know that the energies have been predominantly male up until now, but have recently shifted to the female side.

Men have had to become strong in their role as protectors of the women and the family. Men need to learn to be receptive and cease their domination of the gentle, thinking that the pain they inflict cannot be seen.

"Healers are being called from all over. Women are now taking their place as the original healers around the world, and some of the strongest original healers are starting here in Alaska. So we are seeing not only the shift to the feminine side of leadership, but the women taking their place as healers."

LARRY MERCULIEFF,
AT THE WISDOM-KEEPERS OF THE NORTH
CONFERENCE, *KINDRED SPIRIT* **MAGAZINE**

Everyone sees, but perhaps are just afraid to so. By encouraging women to reform the circle, while the men look after the family, we will re-establish the connections and restore the balance that are vital in this time of history.

SETTING UP A
WOMEN'S DRUMMING GROUP

The drum is a female instrument, since it connects us humans to the rhythm and heartbeat of Grandmother Earth. Drumming in a circle draws women together, letting them find freedom in movement, sound, and voice. The drum draws them away from the fear of their power as the original healers and the keepers of the visions for the future generations.

Form a circle, and let each person have a drum, rattle, or striking sticks. Set no rules and let each person find the instrument that makes them feel good. Ask each

person if they are happy. Even as the drumming is happening, keep a look-out, ensuring that each participant in the group is enjoying her contribution. Have plenty of instruments available so that people can explore.

Start with a short ceremony that will create a sacred space. Keep it light so that everyone feels comfortable and at ease before they start drumming.

Between drumming sessions, have some inspirational readings or give out information so that the people attending can gain an understanding of the purpose of the drumming circle.

Let it become a real circle, with everyone having their say and bringing out the best in everyone.

Invite each person to take turns sitting or lying in the center while the drummers send healing to her.

Encourage people to sing, chant, and move freely.

Powerful things can happen while people are in the circle—be ready to respond to these things.

Be a leader by being available to Spirit, not by domination of the group.

End the evening with a prayer of gratitude to Spirit.

above "We come to you Spirit, we are receptive, we are in need. Come awaken us, we are a circle of your children."

DRUMMING THE MALE CONNECTION

We live in extraordinary times, where the time spiral is winding up and ever-shortening. What we used to do in a day one hundred years ago, we now do in six hours. The day speeds by and flies through the weeks; you work in the office and then before you know it, your children have grown up and flown the nest. What were their names? Did you catch a glance of their spirits as you scurried out before dawn to catch the city train? Are you finding your purpose in this mad race against the clock and this clambering ever upward in your career?

The sweat lodge, vision quest, and sacred pipe are natural ceremonial ways, where men can reconnect to their freedom through cleansing and vision with the spirit guardians of the Sacred Directions, Earth Mother, Grandfather Spirit, and all their relations. Men need to find their warrior nature and true purpose within their lives. They can do this by doing certain things in a certain way and together with other like-minded individuals.

DRUMMING THE MALE ENERGY

This ceremony can be done on your own or together with other like-minded friends. Go to a place in nature to which you feel a strong link.

Stand in a circle and start drumming.

Face and pray or sing to the Sacred Directions.

Turning to face the center, breathe and drum into your base chakra, at the base of the spine.

Become aware of the energy there. Let the drumming bring your feelings out, go wild, and feel the power of your masculine yang energy pouring through. Sing a song and let your voice reach out and release inhibition from within the body. Feel for your animal nature, and let it express itself.

Let your body move as you drum, letting the constraints loosen, making animal sounds and movements.

Turn and face outward, feeling how it feels to be more alone. Drum and sound for a while.

Face into the center again and begin to synchronize the sounds and movement into a feeling of togetherness.

When the drumming stops, it is good to let people talk about their experience by passing a talking stick. Whoever holds the stick talks, no one interrupts, and the others listen. Let Great Spirit talk through you.

A PERSONAL EXPERIENCE
OF MALE POWER

It is coming up to winter solstice, and my friend Terry and I are getting ourselves ready for a "spirit walk," which is a walk with a spiritual purpose. We have our medicine tools, warm clothing, simple food, water, matches, and fire-making materials. We start by meeting up at the sacred grove of yew trees. It is dark and cold when we arrive, but other brothers have already built a fire, so we spend a short time in greetings and enjoying the warm blaze among the trees. Then we sit down by the Medicine Wheel and settle into drumming and praying to the Sacred Directions. When ready, we put the fire out and begin our walk. It is eight miles as the crow flies to Pitch Hill, a steep escarpment facing south, which has been used for eons as a place to greet the midwinter sunrise. We walk through the darkness along bridleways and footpaths, following our noses and feeling our way through the undergrowth. It is really dark and cold and at 3 a.m. all we want to do is sleep. We stop to meditate within the tangled roots of a huge oak tree, feeling its power towering over us. Soon we are moving along again, trudging our way along sleepy lanes and arriving at the hill at 5 a.m. There are two long hours to sunrise and it is damp and very cold. We stir ourselves into action by building a fire, which takes us an hour because of the wet. Sitting by the fire in the cosy hollow, we meditate, drum, and sing. By the time dawn is upon us, we are in deep, silent, connected meditation. There is a thick mist as we perform our ceremony of burying semi-precious stones into the soil on top of the high bluff. A stone, a prayer, and a song for each direction; no one will find these treasures, which are a gift to the earth. We put the fire out and begin our walk home as the birds start to sing and the world comes alive with the hustle and bustle of another morning.

below "We face you, Spirit. We drum and sing to you. Breathe us into oneness. We need your presence in our lives. We face you. Please awaken us."

YOUR NATURAL NAME

You have a natural name that is linked to your purpose on the planet. In Nigeria there is a custom that a pregnant woman is visited by a group of the holy women elders. They put her into a trance and she speaks as the voice of her yet-unborn child. Her voice is high, squeaky, and fast. Through the future mother, the child tells the elders about the gifts, talents, and purpose of its incarnation.

The child is then named before being born, according to this conversation.

So how do you find your natural name? Let me tell you how I found mine, for this may help in your quest. My dear friend Lettie invited me to join her on a journey to Poland. We traveled up to Bialowieza, a huge tract of virgin forest on the Polish–Russian border. There in the

giant oak and pine forests were herds of wild European *wisen*, or buffalo. We were taken by jeep and then we walked, following the herd. Sketching and walking, I soon left the others behind as the herd and I moved ever deeper into the forest. We came to a point where a herd mother stood between the main group of animals and me as they moved on down through the trees. Stopping, I bowed low and honored her, feeling very grateful to be there among the buffalo nation. As I started to sketch her, little rainbows began to radiate like a halo around her head until the whole forest was filled with flickering colored lights. Rubbing my eyes at this natural hallucination, I heard a voice come from the direction of this perfectly still mother of the forest—"This is how I see the forests." The words were repeated over and over, and the lights became less and she moved off following her family. From that time in the huge forest, I have understood the bison family with a deep instinctive knowing.

Three years later, I performed the stone people lodge ceremony with Ed McGaa Eagle Man. Building the lodge before the ceremony, I fell into a ditch and found a *wotai* stone in the perfect shape of a bison's head. During the third part of the ceremony, I asked Eagle Man for my natural name and into the lodge came a herd of buffalo— a vision, sound, and experience that we all heard and felt. There was bellowing and huffing, with hooves scraping the dirt: "*Tatanka Wanagi Wichasta*—Buffalo Spirit Man is your name," announced Eagle Man. Now it is natural for me to feel the attributes of the buffalo nation in keeping

"We receive great gifts from the source of a name; it links us to nature, to the animal nation. It gives power, you can lean on a name, get strength from it."

JOHN FIRE LAME DEER

the family strong, and being a devoted father and husband, feeling that abundance is a quality of life to share, and that being generous and giving to all is extremely important to me.

FINDING YOUR NATURAL NAME

Your natural name helps you fulfill your life purpose, so stay open to how Spirit is going to condense your nature, personality, gifts, and attributes into a name.

Look through your spiritual or third eye into the life around you. You will see how different things are and you will begin to interpret events and happening in a unique way. Observe the direction that attracts you. Follow that direction and watch how *Wakan Tanka* teaches you about your journey of life through the natural world. Ask teachers in the right circumstances to help you find your name. Be happy with the name you are given; feel how it grows on you. Let drumming carry you into feeling your natural rhythms, and feel and look into Spirit while there and ask for your name. It is a process that may take many years. Keep your mind open, and experiences and spirit can manifest your natural name.

left Buffaloes have strong family instincts. No matter what the barrier, if they smell their brothers and sisters, they crash through to join them.

SETTING UP A STONE MEDICINE WHEEL

"With us the circle stands for the togetherness of people who sit with one another, around the campfire, relatives and friends united in peace while the pipe passes from hand to hand."

JOHN FIRE LAME DEER, *LAME DEER SIOUX MEDICINE MAN*

The setting up of a Medicine Wheel, or circle of stones for ceremony, is a spiritual experience that you can do in most wild and tamed areas of this holy earth. Gather together twelve good-sized stones and place them in the center of where you want the Medicine Wheel to be placed. Choose the location carefully by dowsing with a pendulum, hazel, or willow wand, or with copper rods. Find a place where two earth energy lines cross and use this for your central placement. You do not need to be a dowser to do this—if you follow your intuition, you invariably will pick the right place.

To dowse with a pendulum, take a large bead and thread it onto a piece of cotton, swinging it in front of you as you walk toward the area in question. The pendulum swings in the course of least resistance, so if you come to an energy line, it will swing off at a tangent. Follow this line until it crosses another line, then analyze how you feel. Ask your higher self, "Is this going to be a good place

left **Your Medicine Wheel must be in a place that has significance and power to you, and you alone. Remember this.**

to hold a ceremony?" The reply will come as a feeling of discomfort or comfort. The pendulum functions as an amplifier for your intuition.

Smudge the area and yourself with sage and then smudge the rocks. Select from the stones the largest or most appropriate color for each of the cardinal directions and place them in position just outside the main pile.

Starting with the south, lift the stone skyward and make your prayer to the spirit of healing, children, abundance, and humor. Pace out southward twelve paces or feet, depending on how large you feel the circle is to be, and place the stone down in position.

Turning clockwise, return to the center.

Lift up the stone for the west. Hold it up and pray to the spirit of cleansing, insight, water, and your ancestors. Pace out westward and place the stone in position.

Again turn clockwise and return to the center.

Pick up the stone for the north. Lift it up to Grandfather Spirit and make your prayers to White Buffalo Calf Woman, and Mother Mary, for endurance, purity, and wisdom. Pace out to the north and after you have raised the stone to the sky, put it down in its position.

Turn clockwise and return to the center.

Pick up the last of the cardinal stones. Face east, make your prayers to the power of new beginnings, conception, knowledge, and the living teachers. This is the direction of closing the door on the Medicine Wheel. Pace out to the east and place the stone in position.

Check the placement of these primary stone people, their distance and position. Then, starting at the east, place a stone at one o'clock, two o'clock, four o'clock, five o'clock, seven o'clock, eight o'clock, ten o'clock, and eleven o'clock. Again, check on the shape and position of each stone, so that it will feel energetically right.

Look for the face of each stone before you dig a shallow hollow for it to sit in, and make sure the face is turned upward. When you dig, do so carefully and place a small gift of sage or tobacco into the hole.

THE STONE PEOPLE

The stone people are the record-keepers for the Earth Mother. Their consciousness is long and slow. In order to tune into them, you have to slow down to their pace. The Hopi are the keepers of the sacred stone tablets for the sacred red power; these have predictions inscribed on them that foretell the future. The Tibetans have sacred stone tablets secreted in the mountains. In Africa there is a set of black sacred tablets. All around us are sacred stones. Spending some time looking and then meditating with stones is extremely revealing. They are protective, energizing, strong, and comforting, and even have a sense of humor! Place a stone in your left hand, then move it around with your eyes closed until it finds a comfortable position, where it seems to fit. Open your eyes and look on the stone for a face. Again, close your eyes and focus your attention into the face; look in and ask your question.

THE SEASONS, EQUINOX, AND SOLSTICE

"Their relating is perfect, the she and the he,
The Sun Father dances on his lover the sea.
His breath is caressing the mound of her hill,
While the star nations gather,
to time all and fill.
These lovers are perfect, holy earth and the sky.
The moon and the sun move oceans as they fly."

STEVEN ASH

The pulse of the seasons is something we all celebrate in our constant communion with each other. As nations, we rise and fall in mood and behavior, according to the coming rains and snow of winter. And how we blossom as the spring flowers come through in waves of color and scent! We are of the earth, earthly. We are the environment and are not separated from the mother's presence and influence.

The more that we can entwine ourselves with the natural cycles through drumming, chanting, and prayer, the more we weave ourselves into the natural web that is abundance. As the planet turns on her axis, there is a constant balance created between northern and southern hemispheres. One hemisphere warms as the other cools; one day lengthens as the other shortens. The seasons are the north–south cycle that balances the shorter dawn–dusk cycle of east and west. This living layer is so fragile and yet so resilient and the seasons renew, cleanse, and move the stagnation as it occurs.

We can learn to drum the seasons and celebrate their meaning. In the rains and chill of winter, stand beneath the trees that are bare of leaves and find nature's rhythm with two sticks or a rattle. Beat to the sound of the snowfall and drip-drop of rain. Enjoy the fires and the coming-together of enduring and deep companionship.

In spring, drum to the rising of the sap with delicate new leaves, of lambs and wild bird song. Beat the rhythm of conception and birth of nature with growing and expanding knowledge. The cycle of spring always renews. Find its sound in the warm breezes of the lengthening days and the glowing warmth of the radiant sun.

Drum the fullness of summer with total expansion and power, beating outward and upward—the sound of the drum will carry on the dry light air.

Fall is the harvest, decay, and breakdown of the organic abundance of summer. Let your drumming call on the energy of letting go with cleansing and gratitude for all that has been given to you by Spirit.

left When nature's power is manifesting, we can celebrate our connection with pipe and prayer, linking man between heaven and earth.

right Sunset at the fall equinox is an opportunity to welcome in the power of the west, completion, and harvest, saying "thank-you" for all that has been.

Your part in the cycle is now coming to completion. The thirteen moon cycles and the spring and fall equinoxes, combined with the winter and summer solstices, are all times for us to recognize the regular periods of the most intense and concentrated energy. Watch and drum with the phases of the moon.

Celebrate your connection by remembering to rise in the early morning and greet these turning points with dawn meditations. This means that you will now be coordinating your energy input with others on the medicine path. These nodal points act as drumbeats in the annual cycle. By celebrating them, you will be tuning yourself to the drum rhythm of the holy earth and her relationship with the planets and other celestial bodies. We are tiny and insignificant relative to these great cycles, and yet, for some reason, we can have the eyes of appreciation and the ears to listen for beauty. Perhaps this party of life is the creator's gift to us so that we can learn to really appreciate this miracle of life. It is a fact that the power that gives us life can take everything away from us—our home, family, children, arms, legs, or our car. There is only one thing that Spirit cannot take from us and that is our love for Spirit, which is for us to give freely. Drumming with the turning points and welcoming in the seasons concentrates our motives and brings us into the heartbeat of our earth and the universe.

PURIFICATION IN A STONE PEOPLE LODGE

"Inipi—Grandfather's Breath.
I do this because we always purify
ourselves in the Sweathouse before starting
one of our ceremonies. Whether we
celebrate the Sun Dance, or a vision quest,
the 'Inipi' comes first."

JOHN FIRE LAME DEER,
A SIOUX MEDICINE MAN

This is where, with drum in hand, we merge with Spirit in the womb of our sacred mother. We bring together the Sacred Directions and the elements of water, air, fire, and earth. We take ourselves into the darkness within this holy earth den and ask for cleansing with drum, pipe, prayers, and song.

The lodge is a little house made from sixteen hazel or willow saplings, bent and tied to form a beehive shape, which is about chest height. In the center is a hole, into which the hot stones will be placed during the ceremony. The lodge is then covered with blankets, rugs, and tarpaulin so that it is completely dark inside. The door, which is facing west, is in line with an altar of earth and beyond it is the fire in which the stones are being heated.

The day begins with building and covering the lodge and preparing the fire and stones. You can make prayer ties of tobacco, putting the herb into pieces of cloth and tying them onto string while saying your prayers for the world, your family, and friends. You are encouraged to spend time alone, composing yourself, making yourself ready for the ceremony. This is the time to drum and sing, for your prayers to be sincere.

Once the fire is lit, the ceremony begins. Participants may drum and sing around the fire as the rocks heat up. The lodge is smudged with sage. As it gets dark and the stones are red with heat, each person enters the lodge by crawling through the low door and saying, "To all my relations." The fire-keeper, who is the guardian outside the lodge, collects the stones when the lodge leader asks for them to be brought in.

The participants settle in, close to each other, everyone sitting around the hole in the earth. When the hot stones and water are brought in, prayers begin and the door is closed. There are four sections to the stone people or sweat lodge, one for each sacred direction. It is dark and close in the lodge. The rocks are glowing red and faces can be seen on their surfaces. They spit and hiss as water is thrown onto them. Steam and heat, earth and moist air combine with the prayers. These are callings from the dark and the safety of Grandmother's womb, sent out from each person to Grandfather Spirit. When everyone has prayed to the west and perhaps asked for the knowing of his or her spirit guide, the door of the lodge is opened. This is the end of the first endurance.

A drum may be sounded to hold everyone together and keep them earth-centered. More hot stones from the fire, and water are brought in. The second endurance calls to the spirits of the north, for courage and white, cleansing steam. The drum helps to draw in the spirits, which are seen flickering through the lodge like tiny colored lights.

Sometimes a white cloud appears over the stones and extra voices are heard during the singing.

The third endurance calls to the east for knowledge and individual prayer. The leader prays to the attributes of the East and then each of the participants takes it in turn to pray for their particular needs. The beat of the drum continues to send pulsating sound through the prayers, like Grandmother's heartbeat.

The fourth endurance to the south is for the healing of the earth and for healing of relatives and friends who need the intercession of Spirit.

The sweat lodge ceremony concludes with a prayer or song, which is led by the lodge leader.

After the ceremony is finished, everyone sits around the fire and shares their experience with the other members, using a talking stick. Whoever holds the stick, talks while the others listen. After this, shared food is brought out and the day's fast is broken with a late-night feast.

below The lodge is covered; inside, it is as dark as night. It is big enough to sit twenty people who have come to pray in Earth Mother's womb.

bottom Sacred fire heats the rocks so the stone people can speak to us. The path between the fire and lodge is sacred and must not be crossed.

THE VISION QUEST

*"Let me be a free man, free to travel,
free to stop, free to work, free to trade
where I choose, free to choose my own
teachers, free to follow the religion
of my fathers, free to think and
talk and act by myself."*

CHIEF JOSEPH, NEZ PERCE,
TOUCH THE EARTH

YOU WILL NEED

- A tent, sleeping bag, hat, gloves, and warm clothes and boots; be prepared for the cold
- A container of clean drinking water, enough for the duration of your quest
- Your drum, sacred pipe if you have one, a special stone or crystal, plus a notebook or sketch pad
- Something to identify for you the area in which you will hold your vision quest. For example, four short stakes for the Sacred Directions, with tops painted red, yellow, black, and white. Alternatively, create a Medicine Wheel with the stones available when you are out there.

A vision quest is an opportunity to find solitude, and to give yourself the time to be quiet, pray, and to sing, drum, and meditate. Take the time to "touch the earth," and you will find that the earth will listen. Take very little with you; go to a wild and unspoilt place with as little as possible to distract you. You will be fasting, so leave food for when you return. Leave the comforts of home behind and go with the intention of being alone with nature and Spirit. Your drum will be your only companion for sharing songs and prayer.

Start by going out for 24 hours, and build it up next time to 48 hours. Then go for four days and four nights. It is wise to make sure that someone knows where you are going and is keeping an eye on you from a distance, so that if something goes wrong, help is at hand. It is best to choose an experienced person for this. You can also vision quest with others, but find and keep to your own space. It is important to prepare well in advance physically,

emotionally, and spiritually. Find a place where you will not be disturbed by hikers or tourists; it is best to go somewhere high and dry. Tell someone you trust where you will be going. Ask him or her to observe each day and devise a code, which indicates you are safe. Slow down on eating and drinking two to three days before, but have food and dry clothing ready for when you come out.

Carry your equipment to the selected area. Let yourself be guided to the exact position that you feel will fulfill your spiritual and physical needs.

Stake out your area—twelve paces out from the center is a good size—and create sacred space by drumming and praying to the Sacred Directions.

Set up your tent in your staked-out area in such a position that when you are praying at night and walking out from the center toward the Sacred Directions, you will not trip over a guy-rope.

Stay in this area for the duration of the vision quest; do not leave it. You will be tempted, but do not.

Spend the time that you have allocated for the vision quest praying to Spirit with your voice, drum, and tears. With only drinking water and no food, you will get hungry and this will bring up issues that are usually repressed. Sleep only if you have to and use the tent only if and when it all gets too much. Walk the four quarters, watching for what nature and Spirit put in front of you to listen to and observe. This is your opportunity to touch and be touched by Spirit. You are making yourself available to Spirit. Be awake and praying at the turning points—full or new moon, dawn, sunrise, and sunset. Ask, call, and cry to Spirit for a vision to guide you on your medicine path and then trust what is given to you.

left From above, we gain perspective; from below, we are the children of our Earth Mother. Being alone, we pray and make contact with our purpose and vision.

background picture It takes real courage to stay out in nature without food and comforts for four days. The power of nature keeps us humble and receptive.

THE SACRED PIPE

There is a story of how the sacred pipe, or *chanunpa*, came to the native people. It is so extraordinary and beautiful; I will share a shortened version. A sacred woman appeared to two men who were scouting for the buffalo herds because their people were starving. She was *wakan*, a sacred woman; one of the men desired her and she turned him into rotting flesh and bones. She said that she had a message for the people and would come to the tribe the next day to bring it with a special gift. Off like lightning went the remaining hunter to tell the elders the news. They cleaned the place up and got ready. The next day in came this same beautiful maiden, carrying the

"Because this pipe is us. The stem is our backbone the bowl our head. The stone is our blood, red as our skin. The opening in the bowl is our mouth and the smoke rising from it is our breath, the visible breath of our people."

JOHN FIRE LAME DEER

sacred pipe. She instructed the women and men, children and elders on the sacredness of their lives within the tribe and the value of the sacred pipe as a uniting power for the human family. Walking away, she sang these words: "With visible breath I am walking." As she sang, she turned into a white buffalo calf and walked to join the waiting herd of buffalo.

This same beautiful woman features in many cultures: Quan Yin, Isis, Mother Mary, and Our Lady to name but a few. In modern history, she has appeared at Lourdes in France, Fatima in Portugal, San Sebastian de Garabandal in Spain, San Damiano in Italy, and most recently at Medjgorje in Croatia. She most often appears to young children or old women. This same great woman is appearing in different places and giving the same message of peace, wisdom, and connection to the Spirit that White Buffalo Calf Woman gave to the Sioux nation fifteen generations ago with the sacred pipe.

THE SACRED PIPE CEREMONY

It is wise to respect the wishes of the traditional elders, who expect the sacred nature of the pipe to be observed; it is the altar of the people's spiritual belief and experience. The pipe is kept in a protective bag away from curious hands and eyes, and is used only with the correct herbs. Before the sacred pipe ceremony starts, drumming is used to bring the people together and to hold their attention. During the ceremony, the drum is used very discreetly, almost hidden, like a heartbeat, so that everyone can hear the prayers. The pipe represents both the male and the female: the stem, which represents the male, is joined to the bowl representing the female. The pipe is smudged with sage.

Facing west, you make your prayers to the Spirit of cleansing, insight, and the ancestors. As you pray, you put a pinch of tobacco or sacred herbs into the bowl.

left We smudge ourselves and the sacred pipe before we enter ceremony. The sacred pipe contains the prayers of the people.

below left The stone bowl represents the woman, the wooden stem the man. This is a strong pipe, our family pipe, and it brings us into prayer.

Turn to the north and thank White Buffalo Calf Woman for this gift; as you pray, call into the pipe the healing and qualities of courage and endurance when you add in some more of the herb mixture.

Turn to the east and pray, and then do the same for the south. As you pray, beckon in the Spirit and add a pinch of tobacco. Touch the pipe to the holy earth and be grateful; send down your prayers. The tobacco in the pipe bowl represents your intentions.

Reach to the sky and thank Grandfather Sky for the breath we all breathe. Again, add this prayer as a pinch of tobacco. You may want to add some personal prayers and intentions, every time adding some more tobacco.

Now you may smoke the pipe. As you breathe out the white cloud, see the prayers going to Spirit as intended. The pipe is now handed around so others can make their prayers heard and make their breath visible. When the pipe has been smoked, and all the prayers have been said, it is taken apart, cleaned, and put back into its bag.

DRUMMING AND DANCE

"Disease is inertia. Healing is movement.
Shamanic work is about dancing from
within. If you put the body in motion
you will change. You are meant to move:
from staccato, through chaos into lyric
and back into the stillness from which
all the movement comes."

GABRIELLE ROTH, *MAPS TO ECSTASY*

The drum has been the central instrument for movement in all the indigenous cultures from the time before history was recorded. The drum brings the movement out of the earth and out of the air, drawing them together and then expanding them so that they resonate with each person's deep desire to release and explode into expression that comes from within. Dancing with your drum releases tension and stress from the body.

A DRUM AND DANCING EXERCISE

This is an exercise that you can do at home on your own or with others. Dress comfortably for lots of release and movement. Stand up with your drum and get yourself balanced firmly on the earth and then begin beating. Find your rhythm as you close your eyes and let the sound flood over and through you.

Start drumming. Watch your arms and shoulders relax and continue through the body so that every bit of tension in body and mind is released. Then begin to look for movement and follow it, letting all of your tissues follow the movement, finding its regularity, and putting your attention into releasing every fiber of your being into the beating of this rhythm. See this as your beat and instruct all your tissues to recognize it, scanning through your body with your third eye, investigating every "nook and cranny" within the body and ensuring that there is consistency throughout. Keep the beat clean and even.

You may start to shake; it will be a spontaneous experience, so watch for it. This is a self-healing reflex, and when you feel it, go with it. This is your inner knowledge taking the opportunity to release stuck fear from rigid and compressed tissue.

From the releasing zone, begin to release everywhere until your whole body is shaking itself loose, in a chaotic formless way. Keep going until you naturally stop; do not try to stop, but do it as your body feels it. You will see that the drumbeat will be as chaotic as your movement.

As you come out of the chaos, let your body and the drumbeat become soft, easy, and flowing. This is the smoothing out stage, when your creative thought is putting everything back into comfortable order, making sure everything fits into place, now free of stress. Begin to slow down, slow down, and then keep slowing down until every single movement has stopped. Look out for the stillness—this is important. Then let everything begin to center on the breath of the body and let go of any remaining tensions that come to the surface by releasing long sighs or yawns.

Once you are still, with tensions released, stand still like a tree, with your legs strong yet relaxed, and with your torso suspended and totally relaxed in the bowl of your pelvic girdle. Do a final posture check and open your eyes.

below When we drum and dance, we ask Spirit to release our fear so we can be authentic and natural with our expression.

DRUMMING WITH CHANTS AND SONGS

"I really advocate writing your own words, finding a rhythm you like and using the chant to create or call whatever you want into your life, from world peace, to health and happiness."

SHIRLIE RODEN, *SOUND HEALING*

Releasing the voice as you drum is such a joyful act. The drumbeat can draw out the sounds that most people hide away as repressed childhood experiences. These sounds can be brought out into the open and into the safety of the group, where you can hoot, laugh, and spontaneously voice your feelings. How many of you make a stifled little sound every time you think of a past uncomfortable situation? This sound has a root, which needs to be explored, identified with, and then released. Nothing is static. We need to be versatile, almost chameleon-like in nature, adaptable to the ongoing evolution of our personalities, life force, and soul, but having a secure foundation based upon our own experience of inner truth and integrity.

Sounding our truth with the help of the drum is both personal and communal in potential benefit. When you drum and breathe consciously, each beat and each breath is a direct link to Spirit. Then Spirit embodies the sound

and the resulting words and phrases that come through,
and you become an observer of the magnificent! It is a
gift for the moment, something so pure and precious that
comes from Spirit through you. It brings heaven to earth;
it is not yours to own, but your truth to experience.

A SOUNDING AND DRUMMING EXERCISE: CLEANSING

Stand with your drum and start beating your rhythm.
Get settled and bring your focus down into your belly
and on down to between your feet.

Sound three breaths as the lowest tone you can make,
deep down into Grandmother Earth.

Bring your attention up into the base chakra, which is
at the base of the spine and is red like a rose. Sound three
breaths slightly higher in tone than before.

Move up again to the belly chakra, which is orange like
a marigold. Sound three breaths rising in tone.

Rise up again to the solar plexus or stomach chakra and
focus three breaths, visualizing the yellow of a dandelion;
the sound rises slightly again.

Come up to the heart chakra, and focus on a pink rose.
Open up the voice and the drumming and focus on the
heart sound for three breaths.

Bring the sound and attention up to the throat chakra,
which is light blue like the sky. Focus for three breaths.

Concentrate the sound and the attention into the dark
blue of the third eye, which is between the eyebrows.
Clear the space with three even higher breaths of sound.

Move the sound up to the crown, where a violet flame
is blazing, and open up with the breath three times.

Lift the sound up above the head, and visualize white,
then silver, and finally golden light pouring down from a
nine-pointed star in the heavens. Now play with the
sound, using your inner vision to look, sound, and clear
all of your internal space.

RATTLES AND FLUTES

RATTLES

A rattle is a powerful instrument that can be used with the drum or on its own. It is very effective in healing ceremonies where there is stuck energy; the rattle shifts and transforms, helping the process to move forward. When rattling, it is easy to vary the sound for different results.

When shaken hard and with force, the rattle has the ability to shake and loosen up the awareness. When shaken gently, it is soothing and helps you sleep. When shaken very fast, it produces a feeling of expectation.

When shaken in an erratic yet searching way, it can be used to diagnose energy blocks in the aura or human energy field. The rattle can be used for clearing unwanted energy, in the same way as smudging. By working into the area of disturbance and shaking the rattle vigorously with the purpose of cleansing, the rattle enables you to concentrate your intention, its vibrations, and noise shaking away even the nastiest of spirits.

Very fast rattling brings on a trance state. The pace needs to be very rapid and consistent, with no breaks or counter-rhythms in the rattling.

When used as a drum with very gentle tapping, the rattle is excellent for holding the sacred space during prayers and ceremony. The intense and high-pitched sound of the rattle greatly affects the head, whereas the drum, because it is more closely connected with the earth, has a greater affect on the body.

The rattle is very convenient in size and so can easily be carried as a replacement for the drum. Unlike the drum, the rattle is unaffected by water and damp. In an outside ceremony when it is raining hard, the rattle is a good friend to have as an alternative to the drum.

FLUTES

The wooden flute is a magical instrument, very simple to play, and easy to carry with you. It gives a sound totally individual to the soul of the person that plays it. The flute pulls and invites the soul to open, and in nature it can be used to create a strong feeling of safety for animals and plants. It is a wonderful instrument for contacting the plant and animal spirits that hear and sense the quality of the person playing through the instrument. The flute has a vibration of communication that goes beyond and is different from the human vocal scale. The most bewitching and enchanting melodies and tunes can be aroused, drawn out of the ethers and the atmosphere of the place you are in. You can travel into the past, stay happily in the present, or find yourself plucking words, melodies, and information from the future. In sound the wooden flute is the nearest instrument to a flower.

The shape of the human energy form, which has seven major chakras, is very similar to the flute, the flute having six holes that give seven clear notes. When you play the flute, your true self comes out. The flute is used for courtship and healing, and works well with the drum since the flute caresses the soul and the drum steadies and anchors us to the holy earth.

There are four types of flute that I recommend and use: the bamboo side flute, clear and clean like water; the Native American flute, which has a very soft, woody sound; the penny whistle, high and wonderful in woods; pan pipes are breathy and close in sound to the holy earth. You will have to experiment and try out various flutes before you find the one instrument that sings your song even before you touch it.

far left **A flute makes melodies that soothe the heart and soul, break open hardness, and let love and trust replace fear.**

below **The rattle is a powerful medicine tool, pushing away stagnation, helping the energy to flow in the valleys of life.**

CREATING SONGS

Sacred songs can carry the message of healing into the individual as well as into a community. When a melody and lyrics synchronize, they carry power; power to shift blocks in the emotions and power to wash away sorrow. Sacred songs can come from your connection to nature, by developing and deepening your relationship with Spirit, and through your interaction and compassion in relation to others who are in need.

In the past, I found that music and words would have to exist together in my mind for them to work. The song and melody would then fit like a hand in a glove. It starts from a feeling, which turns into a melody, and then within the melody I search for words that fit. If the music and

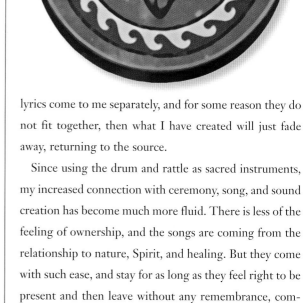

lyrics come to me separately, and for some reason they do not fit together, then what I have created will just fade away, returning to the source.

Since using the drum and rattle as sacred instruments, my increased connection with ceremony, song, and sound creation has become much more fluid. There is less of the feeling of ownership, and the songs are coming from the relationship to nature, Spirit, and healing. But they come with such ease, and stay for as long as they feel right to be present and then leave without any remembrance, coming as gifts for the moment. It is a wonderful experience that takes a lot of focus and trust, especially in a ceremonial situation where there are many people and it is easy to get nervous. You just have to stay focused on Spirit and allow trust to take over.

When creating songs, drum and create a sacred space. By now, it will have almost become second nature to give honor to the Sacred Directions.

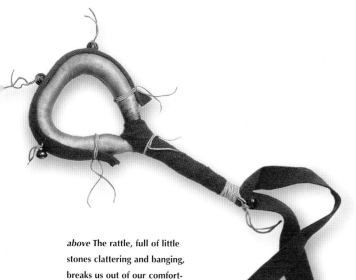

above The rattle, full of little stones clattering and banging, breaks us out of our comfortable stagnant sleep, bringing to the surface hidden pain.

Focus into the sound of the drumming and call Spirit to connect you to the source; as this happens, there is a strong feeling of gratitude and it is from this feeling that a tune and then words spring. In fact, it is just like opening a spring of fresh bubbling water, and you just enjoy its presence moving through. Open your mouth and let the sound come out; then follow it.

Stay open to watching for changes. You might find that from underneath there comes another song—this time a healing song that is specific to one of the group or a chant to which everyone can contribute.

This is guided work, so do not question what is going on, just flow along with the music and words until they stop. You are making yourself available to Spirit in the most connected and channeling form possible.

At the end of a ceremony, always give thanks aloud to the source from where the music is coming, as this eliminates ego from the equation.

I have enjoyed this Sacred Drumming prayer. Every page has been drummed out, Spirit has been invited in, and Spirit has helped me put these words out to make this a book that gives a real message, fitting into our needs at this colossal turning point in history.

In these times, we all need to help each other stay connected to the source. Drumming can help us do that. Our children also need a connection to Spirit that is earthy, sound, and fun. Where will they get it from, if not from us? Where will we get it from, if not from us? For all my relations—*ho, mitakuye oyasin*.

above The tiny stones in this rattle come from the ant hill. There are 405 of them, each taken out carefully by hand.

left top The blue man energy of greed will be erased by the spirit of the women, who drum together in strength.

AUTHOR BIOGRAPHIES

Steven Ash was born in Cornwall, Britain, in 1951. At the age of six, he went with his family of six other brothers and sisters to live on Native American reservations in Canada. Wikwemikong, or Wiki, on Manitoulin Island on the north shore of Lake Huron and Oshwegan, Brantford, Ontario, became their home for the next 2½ years. His father, Dr. Michael Ash, was the reservation doctor. Steven became the apprentice to his father, learning healing and natural medicine. He started creating healing songs at the age of 16 and went on to learn the guitar, flute, and drum. In 1977 he traveled through North America, teaching natural medicine and meeting with Native American teachers. He has lived and studied with Ted Williams, Chief and Medicine Man for the Raven Tribe. He was given the name of *Tatanka Wanagi Wichasta*, or Buffalo Spirit Man, and given the honor of being a pipe carrier by Ed McGaa, Eagle Man. He has learned with Grandfather Wallace Black Elk and has for the last six years been part of a team working within Stonehenge in England to heal the earth's energetic grid. Steven now lives and works as a healer in the south of England with his Austrian wife Renata and their two children, Joy and John.

Renata Ash was born in 1952 in the region of Eastern Tyrol, deep in the mountains of the Austrian Alps. After a very conventional upbringing, her spirit finally broke free when she met Steven at a National Spiritual Healers' Conference in Bexhill, Sussex. With clear instructions from Spirit, she stopped her medical studies at the University of Vienna to move to England, so she could start a family with Steven. In overcoming great personal health problems, she found her way to natural healing and earthbound spirituality, and has been actively practicing Native American spirituality for the past 12 years. Renata has learned with Grandfather Wallace Black Elk and has been involved in energy work within Stonehenge and other sacred sites. She is presently working as a therapist, using music, earth medicine, and shamanic healing practices. Together with her husband, she facilitates ceremonies and rituals to connect people with the power and magic of the Medicine Wheel.

SUPPLIERS AND BIBLIOGRAPHY

UK

Nick Wood, SACRED HOOP MAGAZINE, PO Box 16, Narberth,
Pembrokeshire, SA67 8YG
Tel 01834 860320 Fax 01834 548946
Email nick@sacredhoop.demon.co.uk
Website www.sacredhoop.demon.co.uk

THE SACRED TRUST, PO Box 16, Uckfield, East Sussex, TN22 5WD
Tel 44 (0) 01825 846574
Website www.sacredtrust.org

Terry Webber, MYSTERY MOUNTAIN, Bridge House,
Gomshall, Surrey, GU5 9NP
Tel 01483 202963 Fax 01483 203223
Email info@newage-uk.com
Website www.newage-uk.com

USA

SW USA TREASURES INC, PO Box 65173, Tuscon,
Arizona, 85728 USA
Tel 520 5290755
Email swtreasures@azstarnet.com
Website www.swusatreasures.com

TAOS DRUMS
Website www.webwest.com/taosdrum

LARK IN THE MORNING, PO Box 799,
Fort Bragg, California, CA 95437, USA
Tel 707 964 5569
Website www.larkinam.com

"A Prophecy for Alaska," by Larry Merculieff in *Kindred Spirit*,
    issue 49 (Dartington, UK)
Black Elk, Wallace, and Lyon, William, *The Sacred Ways of a Lakota*
    (Harper Collins, 1990)
Capps, Benjamin, *The Indians* (Time Life Books, 1970)
Erdoes, Richard, and Lame Deer, John Fire, *Lame Deer Sioux
    Medicine Man* (Davis-Poynter, 1973)
Gibran, Kahlil, *The Prophet* (William Heinemann)
Gienger, Michael, *Crystal Power, Crystal Healing* (Blandford Press, 1998)
Gore, Belinda, *Ecstatic Body Postures* (Bear & Co., 1995)
Kharitidi, Olga, *Entering the Circle* (Thorsons, 1996)
Lame Deer, Chief Archie Fire, *The Lakota Sweat Lodge Cards*
    (Dancing Books)
Maharaji, *Reflections* (Visions International, 1989)
Mails, Thomas E., *Fool's Crow* (Bison Books, 1990)
—*The Hopi Survival Kit* (Penguin, 1997)
McGaa Eagle Man, Ed, *Eagle Vision* (Four Directions Publishing)
—*Mother Earth Spirituality* (Harper Collins, 1989)
McLuhan, T.C. (ed.), *Touch the Earth* (Abacus, 1971)
Meadows, K., *Shamanic Experience* (Element 1991)
Medicine Eagle, Brook, *Buffalo Woman Comes Singing* (Ballantine Books)
Neihardt, John G., *Black Elk Speaks* (Bison Books, 1979)
Ortiz, John, *The Tao of Music* (Newleaf, 1997)
Roden, Shirley, *Sound Healing* (Piatkus, 1999)
Roth, Gabrielle, *Maps to Ecstasy* (Harper Collins, 1989)
Sams, Jamie, *Sacred Path Cards* (Harper Collins, 1990)
Seattle, Chief, *Brother Eagle, Sister Sky, a Message from Chief Seattle*
(Hamish Hamilton)
—*How Can One Sell the Air? Chief Seattle's Vision* (The Book Publishing
    Company. 1992)
Starck, Marcia, *Women's Medicine Ways* (The Crossing Press, Freedom,
    California, 1993)
Tame, David, *The Secret Power of Music* (Turnstone Press Limited)

CHAPTER FIVE

HOW TO DRUM

This section of *Sacred Drumming* gives you the practical tips that will help you incorporate drumming into your life.

It is assumed that you will be using a Native American hand drum, which is either struck with your hand or a soft-ended drumstick called a beater. You will learn how to hold the drum and how to produce different nuances of sound using both the beater and your hand.

With the Native American hand drum, the beater is an essential item and we will take a detailed look at its use, giving you as many options in sound and technique as possible. We will walk you through the process of creating rhythms with different types of drums and rattles, and show you how to adapt your drumming techniques to differing qualities of both physical space and personal feeling.

Lastly we will explore each track on the CD, and analyze its content so that you can follow its style and technique on your own. A simple score is provided to help you follow the tracks.

PRACTICAL INFORMATION

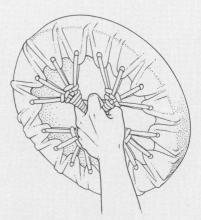

Hold the "cross" at the back of the drum with your left hand if you are right handed. Remember to get a firm yet relaxed grip.

How to hold the drum

• If you are right handed, hold the "cross" (the center of the back of the drum, where the strings meet) with your left hand. If you are left handed, hold the cross with your right hand (reverse the instructions if you are right handed). Get a good grip, but make sure that you are also relaxed so that the whole drum can move with the rhythm of the beat. Sacred drumming is not a static experience and you may want to move around as you beat your drum. The cross is the fulcrum around which you lift and lower your drum. Make sure that this cross is comfortable. If necessary, bind some soft chamois leather around the cross strings so that your hand is comfortable and your grip is secure. This is especially important if you are using a large drum.

• Keep your drum level with your heart as much as possible, so that the sound will resonate in your chest cavity. This will give you a much better sense of beat. When you hold the drum, the skin surface should be perpendicular to the ground, not face up or face down. This way, your right hand—which is holding the beater—will move across your chest, making contact with the drum surface in front of your heart area.

• Relax and use your whole body to keep the beat. The more you can relax every part of your body, the more even and steady your drumbeat will be. Get into the habit of keeping a steady and even tap with your right foot.

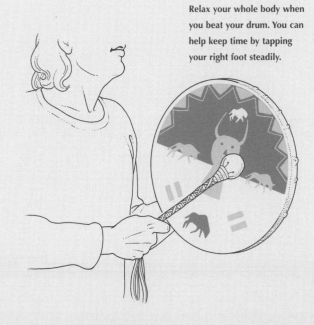

Relax your whole body when you beat your drum. You can help keep time by tapping your right foot steadily.

You can easily make a beater yourself using a piece of wood and some animal skin.

The beater

The beater (or drumstick) is made from a piece of wood about half an inch (2 cm) in diameter (about the width of a finger) and 12 inches (30 cm) in length (the distance from fingers to elbow). A ball of cloth covered with soft leather is tied over the wood at one end. The whole stick is sometimes bound with soft leather for comfortable handling.

Holding the beater

Traditionally, the beater (or drumstick) is held at the skinny end, the point furthest from the soft end. This holding position will produce the loudest sound and will facilitate clear, even beating.

Holding the beater one third up from the end

Holding the beater in this position produces a clear, strong sound and the balance of the stick assists you in keeping a steady, constant beat. It feels natural and comfortable and helps you sustain your drumming for longer periods of time.

Holding the beater at the point of balance

This technique is for the advanced drummer who wants to produce a more complex and interesting sound. Find the middle of the beater (or drumstick)—the point of balance. Begin beating the middle of the drum. As you beat, move toward the rim, so that the end of the stick makes contact with the opposite rim. This will produce two beating sounds, one from each end of the stick. You can then move the beater back toward the center, getting the single deeper beat again. By moving backward and forward on the skin, you not only get a double beat but you can also change the pitch and rhythm of the drum from low single beats to high double beats.

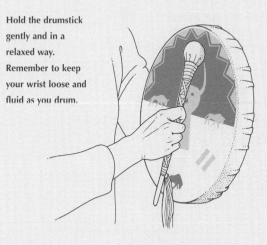

Hold the drumstick gently and in a relaxed way. Remember to keep your wrist loose and fluid as you drum.

How to vary the sound of the drum

There are many ways to change the timbre of the drum. We describe three simple methods of dampening the drum so that a dull, more muffled sound can be gained. This is sometimes necessary when you drum in a confined space and may be useful in your home, when you do not want to disturb the neighbors late at night.

1 As you hold the cross, stretch your middle finger into the drum so that it makes contact with the skin. Beating on the position where the finger is making contact from behind will produce a duller sound. The harder you press against the skin the higher the timbre, because the skin becomes tighter and more stretched. Generally a higher timbre also produces a much softer sound.

You can beat the drum with the hand that holds the cross at the back. This generally produces a more muffled sound.

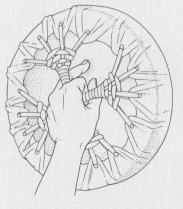

2 As you beat the drum, lower the rim of the drum until it touches the ground—the sound will become less bright as the vibrations are absorbed into the earth.

3 You can produce a slow yet strong meditative beat with a dull muffled sound by holding the beater in the middle or balance point of the stick

Move the beater toward the edge of the drum for a difference in sound—it will be higher and much brighter.

with the fingers rather than in the palm of the hand. Pivot the end of the drumstick on the rim of the drum; as the stick maintains contact with the drum, the sound is muffled. This is used for gentle, quiet times, where the drum holds the energy like a heartbeat (CD Track 4).

How to increase the volume

The loudest sounds can be obtained by beating the center of the skin. This is also the place where the sound is deepest and fullest. The center of the drum surface is the meeting point where all the vibrations travelling through the skin come together. At times these vibrations become so intense they will almost cause you to miss the beat. For general drumming, and especially while you are still a beginner, it is better to drum just off center, where the skin is not moving as much. As you move the beater (drumstick) toward the rim, the sound will become higher, brighter, and more hollow, as the tension of the skin is greater. There is a position approximately two thirds in from the rim, where the true note of your drum can be found. Like every instrument, your drum also has a special resonant vibration. Try to experiment by moving the beater in from the rim as you drum so that you can find these different sounds. Some drums, especially ones that are played often, have a special area where the sound is exceptional—clear and mellow. As you experiment with your drum, you will notice this place of optimum sound.

Drumming with the drumstick and hand

This is similar to the dull meditation drumbeat described above. Hold the stick in the middle between the thumb and first finger and pivot its end against the rim of the drum. As the stick makes contact with the skin, allow the pads of your fingers to beat the drum. Hit the drum in different areas to produce a variety of sounds; these vary from dull thuds to beautiful ringing sounds similar to the sound produced by Tibetan singing bowls. With practice you can draw out and emphasize this ring so that eventually this high resonance overlays the drumbeat.

Drumming with the fingernails

The fingernails give a very sharp, almost clacking sound on the drum's surface.

1 If you use all the fingers together, you will be able to draw out the ringing resonance that we

Tap the drum with your fingernails to get attention with the sharp, crisp sound.

got in the previous technique. I use this fingernail drumming to break up stagnation or to bring back focus if people become distracted.

2 When you make contact with the drum surface with one fingernail at a time, starting with the little finger, followed by the ring, middle, and lastly the index finger, you can get a roll that sounds like horses' hooves galloping across the plains. Again, take the time to explore the different areas and sounds over the drum surface.

Drumming the rim with the drumstick

Drumming on the rim of the drum gives a lovely "woody" noise, which is a nice contrast to the other sounds. When the rawhide-covered wooden rim is struck with the shaft of the drumstick, a whole variety of sounds can be made, from dull pattering through to sharp ringing and loud clacks. The quality of the sound again depends on the point of contact between drum and stick.

Drumming with the palm of the hand produces a soft and resonant sound which is very soothing.

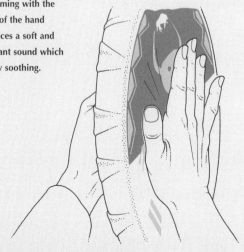

Drumming with the hand

Drumming with the palm of the hand is one of the most frequently used and valuable techniques. The reasons for this are:

• It produces a softer, more persuasive tone.

• Feeling the contact with the sound through the palm of the hand makes you very sensitive to the relationship between you and your drum.

• It is the one time where you can hold the drum up to your face and feel the vibrations and beat going directly into your head.

• With the drum on your lap you can explore drumming with both hands. When you drum with your left hand, you activate the right hemisphere of the brain, which is the creative side. When you drum with your right hand, you activate the left hemisphere of the brain, the analytical side. Drumming with both hands will help you balance your intuitive, artistic, and logical aspects.

Drumming with a rattle

Using the rattle to create different rhythms is a lovely experience. If you are drumming alone and want the sound of the rattle as well, either strap the rattle handle to the drumstick with a piece of leather or hold both handles together. The handle of the rattle should be far from the drum, so when the skin is struck by the drumstick, the rattle will also produce sound. You can even alternate the sound, shaking the rattle into the air on its own, then joining it with the drumbeat. Another technique is to hold the drumstick at the point of balance. Then you can move from a single beat into the double beat where the end of the stick hits the rim of the drum, and then further expand the sound by adding to it the sharp hiss of the rattle.

Drumming with stones in the drum

Put some small pieces of wood, shell, or stones inside the drum. As you beat the drum they will rattle away and create a humming reverberation. These vibrations will seem to fill in the spaces between the drumbeats.

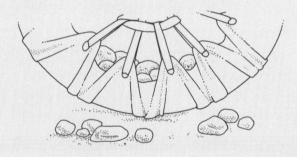

POSITIONS AND PLACES

Standing

Stand with your feet shoulder-width apart. Bend and soften your knees and allow yourself to lean gently forward so that the weight of your body is carried by the muscles of your legs rather than the bones. Often it helps to call into your mind the picture of a strong tree trunk and then adapt your posture accordingly. Relax your shoulders, chest, and abdomen. Hold your drum up at chest height and feel for the rhythm of the drumbeat through your whole body.

Sitting

If you prefer to drum sitting on a chair, make sure that you sit with your back straight and make contact with the ground through your feet. There

Stand with awareness when you are drumming. Imagine you are a strong, tall tree reaching up to the sky and beyond.

should be a 90-degree angle at your ankles, knees, and lower back. Sit erect, balanced and relaxed. If you are outside, either sit cross-legged, squat, or kneel, sitting back on your feet. It is important to get the posture right, so you feel comfortable when you drum, especially when you are in ceremony. If you are drumming in a group, attune your activities to those of the group so that you are working as a team.

Dancing

Dancing while drumming is a natural and joyful experience. We often find that when we dance and drum, the drum and beater are moving together as if we were clapping our hands—they are both moving in and out with the beat. Again, start by

Sit with your back straight when you drum sitting down, and make sure that your feet are in contact with the earth.

Dancing and drumming go together naturally, just like clapping the hands. Don't feel self-conscious, just go with the rhythm!

holding the drum level with the heart, but in your dance you may want to lift the drum or lower it. Move and weave on your beat.

Drumming outside

Gaining the confidence to drum outside in nature is a real step forward. This is the best place to practice, because through your connection with the drum you will find an increasing awareness of nature and everything that is around you.

It is important to be aware that extreme weather conditions can damage a drum. Excess heat from the sun can cause the skin to tighten and warp the wooden frame; once the frame is misshapen the drum will have a buzzing sound when it is struck because the skin no longer has good contact with the frame. Never leave your instrument exposed in the back of a car or in direct sunlight. Wetness and dampness will slacken the skin and may warp the frame. If your drum does get wet, dry it slowly at room temperature so it can resettle into its old shape. If you dry it too quickly, there may be irreparable damage and your drum will only be useful as a wall decoration.

Carry your drum in a waterproof bag and keep it in the shade when you are not using it. To get a good sound, you may have to put the drum in the sun or near to a fire to tighten the skin if it has lost tension because of a damp environment. The drum bag is also useful to sit on when you are drumming outside, so we would definitely encourage you to get one or make one yourself.

Walking

It is an exhilarating experience to walk in nature while you drum or rattle. You can set a pace with the drum that will allow your whole body to move with much greater ease. This is also a great opportunity to practice keeping even time, to create songs, or to get in touch with nature. Long beats will allow you to move easily and in a relaxed manner, which is perfect for walking through flat or less interesting terrain. The ground is covered steadily to the long, slow beat and the walk can become a meditation. A fast, steady, and strong beat is exceptional for getting up the slopes of hills and mountains. The drumbeat will lead you through exhaustion and tiredness, drawing your attention away from the pain of straining muscles.

On long walks you will find that a rattle—being generally smaller and lighter than a drum—is an indispensable travelling instrument.

Walking with your drum can be an exhilarating experience. Get a partner or friend to carry a rattle as well.

DRUMMING WITH THE CD

TRACK 1

DRUMMING THE SACRED DIRECTIONS

First listen to Track 1. It has a straight 1-2-3-4 beat with no accents. (These are beats that are given more emphasis than others.) In ceremonial drumming it is important that you keep the beat even; do not put an accent on the first beat. The Native American teachers call this "Hollywood drumming;"; it is what you hear in the cowboy films in the 1960s. So keep the beat steady and regular, 1-2-3-4 not **1**-2-3-4.

Start by facing South and begin beating your drum to the rhythm of 1-2-3-4. When you hear the flute play seven bars of melody, it is time to sing the song of the Sacred Directions, which is sung four times when the humming starts.

"Spirit of the South, Spirit of the South,
Bring me healing and laughter."

The voice part is then followed by a piece of drumming; during this time you should make your prayers to the power of the South, either silently as you drum or out loud. As the sound of the drums changes you turn sunwise (clockwise) and face West. Drumming to the West, you wait for the flute to cue you into the humming part where you sing:

"Spirit of the West, Spirit of the West
Bring me cleansing and insight."

Again make your prayers to the West over the drumbeat that follows.

Keep turning through the medicine wheel clockwise while you are drumming, singing, and praying to each direction. Here are the words for the North, East, Earth, Sky, and Spirit:

"Spirit of the North, Spirit of the North
Bring me wisdom and purity."

"Spirit of the East, Spirit of the East
Help the new dawn in me rising."

"Grandmother Earth, Grandmother Earth
You give me food and shelter."

"Grandfather Sky, Grandfather Sky.
You breathe the breath of life into me."

"Spirit of within, Spirit of within
You are my appreciation."

It is best to learn the words from the text as you listen to the CD and then practice singing and drumming over the recorded sound.

An extended piece of drumming toward the end of the track gives you the opportunity to offer more prayers. Drumming along with this piece will also help you learn to keep a steady, prayerful beat. The flute comes in again as an introduction to the last part of the words:

"Wakan Tanka, Great Spirit, O Great Mystery,
Take the veil of ignorance away from me.
Wakan Tanka, Great Spirit, O Great Mystery
Take the veil away so I may see."

SKILLS YOU WILL LEARN FROM TRACK 1
• **Keeping the drumbeat even without any accent.**
• **Drumming a steady beat while singing and praying out loud.**

TRACK 2

CLEARING AND CLEANSING SPACE

Listen to this a number of times until you begin to understand the music. As we drum, imagine that you are walking through a house, going into corners and around tables, into closets and dark spaces. Where the energy is clear (where you feel no obstacles or "stickiness" in the air about you) the beat is a steady 1-2-3-4. When we come upon stagnation or disturbing energy this will need to be cleared. Here the rattle goes wild and the drumbeats into a frenzy. The wild beat breaks up the energies that need to be moved. Then we come to a still place and the drumbeat drops to a whisper until again we come across a place of disturbance and the rattle and drum pushes the energy out of the way to clear the space.

As you drum for clearing, imagine the beat of the drum and the hiss of the rattle cleansing the area.

SKILLS YOU WILL LEARN FROM TRACK 2
•**Perfecting the drumming techniques described earlier.**
•**Drumming the drum rim.**
•**Dampening the drum sound.**
•**Drumming and rattling at the same time.**
•**Driving and strong drumming to push out stagnation.**
•**Trusting your intuitive impressions about the quality of space and energy and then allowing your intuition to guide you into the right use of drum and rattle.**

TRACK 3

MEDICINE AND HEALING

At first this track will sound very similar to Track 2, but there is a basic difference. When you drum to clear space, you imagine that the sound is pushing outward, whereas for medicine and healing drumming, you imagine the sound is pushing inward. The person awaiting healing should sit on a chair facing the Sacred Direction that corresponds with the healing qualities that they are asking for (*see pages 34–49*).

You should move around them, beating your drum and intuitively drumming away stagnation and sending in love through the drum sound.

As you work on the various areas of the body you may feel inspired to sing, so allow this to happen. Other drummers could support you with a steady grounding beat with no accent. Other healers may be present as you work with your drum.

SKILLS YOU WILL LEARN FROM TRACK 3
- **Sending healing through the drum.**
- **Drumming and singing spontaneously.**
- **Seeing a person's needs through medicine drumming.**

TRACK 4

MEDITATING WITH THE DRUM

Studies have shown that meditating on the heartbeat effectively reduces stress. It is a simple 1-2, 1-2, 1-2, 1-2 beat with no accent. Before you start, feel your pulse on the wrist and use that as the basic rhythm on which to base your meditation. Keep it slow and breathe into the sound. You might want to rest your drumstick on the rim as a pivot or drum with the palm of the hand as well as the drumstick.

On this track, Tibetan singing bowls add to the richness of sound and the ethereal quality of the meditation experience. In your own practice, feel free to incorporate any additional instruments you feel may be useful. You will soon discover whether an instrument helps deepen the meditation or, alternatively, becomes a distraction. At all times follow your own feelings and intuition. You can also work with other drummers using this track, and meditate as a group. This is a valuable lesson on learning to drum with other people.

SKILLS YOU WILL LEARN FROM TRACK 4
- **Keeping a steady heartbeat rhythm.**
- **Working with others and gentle drumming.**
- **Listening to others drum.**
- **Creating a sacred space ready for ceremony.**

TRACK 5

GROUP DRUMMING

Group drumming is your opportunity to let go! It also gives others room to be heard. Every person drums differently and has different skills. If everyone wants to be heard at the same time, a cacophony will be produced, so agree that everyone takes a turn in leading the drumming.

For group drumming it is best to sit or stand in a circle, to share the sound with others in the group. It is an opportunity to work with others, to create wonderful rhythms, and to harmonize your sound with those sitting across the circle from you.

SKILLS YOU WILL LEARN FROM TRACK 5

•**Drumming in a team.**

•**Listening to others.**

•**Gaining confidence from drumming a strong common beat.**

Drumming with other people helps you gain confidence in your own sound and drumming abilities.

TRACK 6

MEDICINE SONG

This is a Medicine Song, where drum, voice, and flute are weaving together and holding beat, rhythm, and melody. On this track you will hear some accentuated beats, 1-2-3-4, that are fine for songs, but are not suitable for ceremony. Why? This section is too short. The section on Track 1 is quite long, but they get shorter and shorter—try to keep length consistent.

SKILLS YOU WILL LEARN FROM TRACK 6

•Working with accents on the first beat.

•Using your voice and drum at the same time.

•Varying the drum to fit voice and then flute.

TRACK 7

TRANCE DRUMMING

Trance drumming is extremely fast, about 300 beats a minute, with no accent and no breaks. The beat is held on a rattle or drum or both. It must be continuous for at least 15 minutes to be effective. It purposefully breaks you away from all distractions, thoughts, and memories. The drumming on this track creates a safe space while helping you achieve a change in consciousness. It also acts as your anchor, allowing you to find your way safely back into your reality from your journey to other dimensions of space and time. You can stand, lie, kneel, or sit to listen to this track. You can also practice this drumming technique to explore different levels of consciousness.

SKILLS YOU WILL LEARN FROM TRACK 7

•**Holding a steady fast trance beat.**

•**Discipline and strength as a drummer.**

YOU AND YOUR DRUM

Enjoy your drumming and make it a personal odyssey to love and care for your drum, and use it in the way that it should be. If you spend time alone with your drum, you will come to know it as a living being, and this relationship will help your drumming become even more real. After you have learned the basics of drumming, it is up to you to explore the potential of your own drum—both by yourself or in a group of other drummers. It is best to spend time alone with your drum before playing it with others, so you can become more confident about your drumming. Love your drum and it will sing out its love for you, its owner and keeper.

Trance drumming can be physically and mentally demanding. You can lie down to drum if you prefer.

INDEX